THE ART OF FLY TYING

THE HUNTING & FISHING LIBRARY®

By John van Vliet

JOHN VAN VLIET grew up fly fishing in the Adirondack Mountains of upstate New York, and honed his skills on the spring creeks of southeastern Minnesota. An accomplished flytier and fly-fishing instructor, he has written extensively on fishing for trout.

CY DECOSSE INCORPORATED

A COWLES MAGAZINES COMPANY

Chairman/CEO: Bruce Barnet
Chairman Emeritus: Cy DeCosse
President: James B. Maus
Executive Vice President: William B. Jones

THE ART OF FLY TYING

Author and Book Development Leader: John van Vliet
Hunting & Fishing Library Director: Dick Sternberg
Technical and Photo Advisor: Chad M. Peterson
Editors: Janice Cauley, Dick Sternberg
Project Manager: John van Vliet
Assistant Project Managers: Carol Harvatin, Tracy Stanley
Senior Art Director: Bradley Springer
Art Directors: Geoffrey Kinsey, Dave Schelitzche
Photography Production Coordinator: Cathleen Shannon
Director of Photography: Mike Parker
Studio Manager: Marcia Chambers
Principal Photographers: Cy DeCosse, Mark Macemon
Staff and Contributing Photographers: Stuart Block, David H. Funk, Rebecca Hawthorne, Rex Irmen, William Lindner, Paul Najlis, Charles Nields, Tony Oswald, Mike Parker
Photo Assistants: Steven Hauge, Kevin Hedden, Mike Hehner, Jim Moynagh, Robert Powers, Gary Sandin
V. P. Development Planning and Production: Jim Bindas
Production Managers: Laurie Gilbert, Amelia Merz
Senior Desktop Publishing Specialist: Joe Fahey
Production Staff: Amy Berndt, Kathlynn Henthorne, Elaine Johnson, April Jones, Mike Schauer, Kay Wethern, Nik Wogstad
Illustrators: Thomas Boll, Jon Q. Wright

Cooperating Individuals, Agencies and Manufacturers: The American Museum of Fly Fishing – Alanna Fisher; Tom Andersen; Dan Bailey's Fly Shop – John Bailey; Wayne Bartz; Burger Brothers' Outfitters – Mike Burger, John Edstrom, John Goplin; Fly Fisherman Magazine – John Randolph; H. Gerstner & Sons – Jack Campbell; Dean Hansen; Mark Larson; Metz Hatchery; Bob Mitchell's Fly Shop – Bob & Jean Mitchell; O. Mustad & Sons; J. Rex & Associates – Jim Rex; The Orvis Company – Tim Joseph, Tom Rosenbauer; Partridge of Redditch; Plano Molding Company – Bill Cork; Rodcraft – Dave Peterson; Umpqua Feather Merchants – Ken Menard; Kevin Wible

Printing: R. R. Donnelley & Sons Co. (0994)

Library of Congress
Cataloging-in-Publication Data

van Vliet, John.
The art of fly tying / by John van Vliet.
p. cm. – (The Hunting & fishing library)
Includes index.
ISBN 0-86573-043-1 (hardcover), 0-86573-046-6 (Wire-O)
1. Fly tying. I. Title. II. Series.
SH451.V58 1994   94-12559
688.7'912—dc20

Also available from the publisher:
The Art of Freshwater Fishing, Cleaning & Cooking Fish, Fishing With Live Bait, Largemouth Bass, Panfish, The Art of Hunting, Fishing With Artificial Lures, Walleye, Smallmouth Bass, Dressing & Cooking Wild Game, Freshwater Gamefish of North America, Trout, Secrets of the Fishing Pros, Fishing Rivers & Streams, Fishing Tips & Tricks, Fishing Natural Lakes, White-tailed Deer, Northern Pike & Muskie, America's Favorite Fish Recipes, Fishing Man-made Lakes

Contents

Introduction

Of all the ways to catch a fish, few are as exciting and rewarding as catching one on a fly you've tied yourself. An artificial fly can entice the slow rise of a trout or the explosive strike of a largemouth bass. And for many fly anglers, tying the fly is as satisfying as landing the fish.

For thousands of years, anglers have been wrapping hooks with wool, fur, feathers and thread in order to imitate some morsel in a fish's diet and fool the fish into taking the hook. But despite this long history, the methods and techniques of fly tying remain essentially unchanged.

Fly tying is the craft of combining several basic elements — tail, body, wing and hackle — to create a completed fly. It can be accomplished with a few simple tools and materials. And once you've learned the basics, you'll find that most fly patterns are simple and easy to tie.

The purpose of this book is to introduce you to the fundamentals of fly tying, including the tools, materials and techniques required for tying, and provide you with clear, color photographs of the most popular fly patterns and recipes you need to tie them.

The first section, "Understanding Fly Tying," gives you a brief history of fly tying and its traditions, from the earliest written descriptions to today's innovations in materials.

This section also shows you the wide variety of aquatic insects and other foods that make up a fish's diet and explains how understanding these various aquatic foods can help you tie more accurate and effective imitations.

The second section, "Fly-Tying Tools & Materials," shows you all the tools you'll need to tie flies, and the wide range of hooks, thread and materials available. You'll also learn tips on organizing your work area for more efficient tying.

"Fly-Tying Basics" includes a description of the many components of a fly. You'll learn about each stage of tying a fly, from how to start the thread on the hook to the best finishing knots. In between, you'll find dozens of essential techniques for tying tails, bodies, wings, hackle and other parts of a fly, with each technique shown in full-color, step-by-step photos.

The last section, "Fly Patterns," shows you how to combine these elements to create a finished fly. You'll learn step-by-step procedures for tying six different fly types, including streamers, nymphs, dry flies, wet flies, terrestrials and bass flies.

After each basic pattern, we'll show you photos and complete recipes for dozens of other patterns that can be tied using the techniques demonstrated in the initial step-by-step sequence. In all, you'll learn over two hundred classic and new patterns.

Whether you're just starting or have been tying for years, this book is sure to expand your knowledge and improve your skills in the art of fly tying.

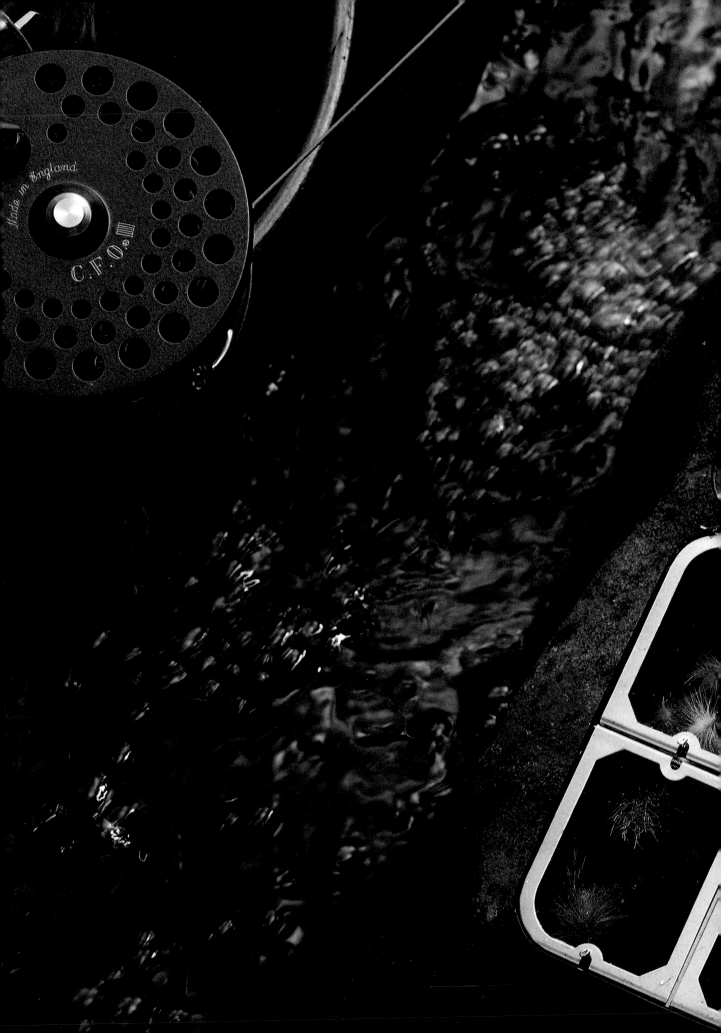

History of Fly Tying

No other aspect of modern sport-fishing is as steeped in tradition and history as tying and fishing artificial flies.

The tools and materials of fly tying are reminiscent of a time when the rewards of a season's hunt — the feathers and furs of game birds and animals — were used to create fly patterns that would catch fish.

While many people credit Izaak Walton and his 1676 edition of *The Compleat Angler* with the beginning of fly fishing, the origins of tying and fishing artificial flies actually date back thousands of years.

The earliest written account appeared in the third century A.D., when the writer Aelianus described a Macedonian method of catching fish using artificial flies:

"They do not use [natural] flies for bait, for if a man's hand touch them they lose their natural color, their wings wither, and they become unfit food for the fish.

"[Instead] they fasten crimson wool around a hook, and fix on to the wool two feathers that grow under a cock's wattles, and which in color are like wax."

Centuries later, in 1496, an Englishwoman named Dame Juliana Berners wrote the popular *Treatise of Fishing with an Angle*, which included a description of dressing a hook with virtually the same materials used by the Macedonians.

In the years between Aelianus and Berners, fishing with an artificial fly had evolved from a practical way to catch fish to a highly refined sport, but the method of winding materials onto a hook remained the same.

Many of today's popular fly patterns call for man-made materials

Interest in fly tying blossomed in the 1880s, as flytiers in Europe, Britain and America were tying both gaudy, fanciful wet flies and increasingly exact imitations of natural insects. But in America, these fancy wet-fly patterns gradually gave way to the more realistic flies, as the native Eastern brook trout was slowly replaced by the brown trout.

The brown, an import from Germany in 1883, was far more selective than the brookie. As a result, flytiers were forced to create patterns that more closely resembled the natural insects that made up the trout's diet.

At about the same time, in 1881, Dr. Henshall's *Book of the Black Bass* introduced artificial flies — many of them traditional trout patterns — to countless bass fishermen.

In the 1950s, the feathers and fur of exotic and endangered species that had once been among the standard fly-tying materials became increasingly difficult to obtain. Flytiers turned to other sources of natural materials, and patterns no longer called for owl, condor or imported jungle cock feathers.

In the 1970s, the introduction of synthetics, such as Antron® and Mylar®, revolutionized fly tying. Colors, particularly fluorescents, that were unobtainable in nature or through dying natural materials, were now available in synthetic threads, dubbing and wing materials.

Today, in an age of man-made materials and high-tech equipment, when fly anglers pursue everything from bass and pike to bonefish and tarpon, the popularity of fly tying shows no sign of diminishing as another generation learns the craft of winding materials onto a hook in order to entice a fish to strike.

HUNDRED-YEAR-OLD fly patterns (left) show the high level of skill and wide range of natural materials employed by flytiers of the time.

Aquatic Insects & Other Foods

One of the secrets to tying effective flies is understanding the foods that fish eat. Trout, for example, rely heavily on aquatic insects for food, explaining why most trout flies resemble some stage in the life cycle of an aquatic insect.

Traditional fly patterns were designed to imitate a small number of species and stages of aquatic insects. Today, there are fly patterns imitating practically all of them, as well as minnows, frogs, leeches, sculpins, crabs, shrimp and many other kinds of aquatic foods.

The majority of fly patterns fall into the category of *imitators.* Many flytiers go to great lengths to "match the hatch," creating precise impressions of a specific stage of a certain insect species.

But some fly patterns are classified as *attractors,* because they are tied in colors and shapes that do not resemble any natural aquatic food. These patterns trigger a fish's defense mechanism or arouse its curiosity, causing it to strike the fly.

Fly types include: (1) attractor, (2) imitator and (3) searching pattern

Yet another category, called *searching patterns,* is used to locate fish. A searching pattern does not resemble any specific natural insect, but rather a broad range of similar insect types. These patterns are best when exploring new water.

The key to successful imitation is knowing what the natural insect looks like. Whenever possible, study the size, shape and color of insect the fish are eating. Many flytiers also observe the action and examine the texture of the insect and use materials that will duplicate them.

Following are the growth stages of the four main groups of aquatic insects: mayflies, caddisflies, midges and stoneflies.

LOOK for streamside insect activity to help you match the hatch. Clouds of emerging or mating insects (above) are an indication of what the fish may be eating. When no insects are visible above the water, turning over submerged rocks (inset) can help you select a nymph pattern.

Growth Stages of Mayflies, Caddisflies, Midges and Stoneflies

Nymph

Dun

Spinner

MAYFLY life stages include the nymph; *subimago*, or dun; and *imago*, or spinner (pp. 12 - 13). All stages have two or three tail filaments. Adults (duns and spinners) have two large upright wings, and some have a set of smaller wings. The wings of mayfly duns are opaque; spinners, transparent.

Larva

Adult

Larva

Adult

CADDISFLIES have no tails and four wings, which are folded tent-style over their bodies when not in flight. The stages of the caddisfly are: larva, pupa and adult. In many species, the larva builds a shell, or case, in which to live. Adults and larvae range in color from tan and cream to olive and dark brown.

MIDGES are generally quite small, with only two wings and no tails. They are found most often in slow-moving water and vary greatly in color. Midges, like caddisflies, mature from larva to pupa to adult. The mosquito is a common type of midge.

Nymph

Adult

STONEFLY nymphs and adults have two short tail filaments. Adults also have four hard, shiny wings that lie flat over the body when not in flight. Stoneflies mature from nymph to adult with no intermediate stage. Some stonefly species are among the largest aquatic insects, although others can be quite small. Many species of stonefly emerge and mate on land, not on the water, returning to the water to lay their eggs.

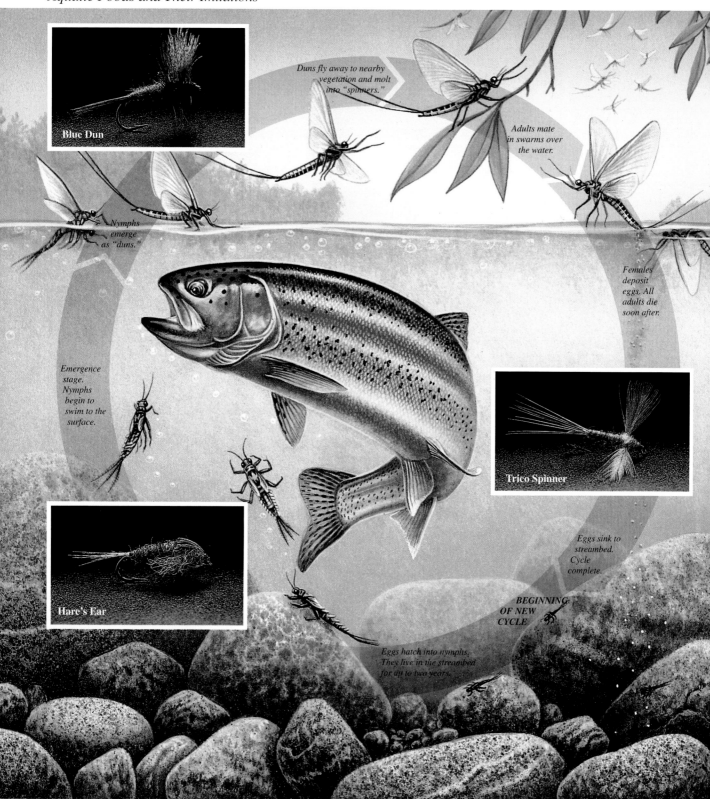

Blue Dun

Duns fly away to nearby vegetation and molt into "spinners."

Adults mate in swarms over the water.

Nymphs emerge as "duns."

Females deposit eggs. All adults die soon after.

Emergence stage. Nymphs begin to swim to the surface.

Trico Spinner

Eggs sink to streambed. Cycle complete.

Hare's Ear

BEGINNING OF NEW CYCLE

Eggs hatch into nymphs. They live in the streambed for up to two years.

MAYFLY LIFE CYCLE. Mayfly eggs hatch into nymphs, imitated by patterns like this Hare's Ear Nymph (inset). This stage lasts from a few months up to two years, then the nymphs ascend to the surface and hatch, or *emerge*, as duns. This stage is imitated by dry-fly patterns like this Blue Dun (inset). Duns then fly up into the streamside vegetation, where they shed their skin, or *molt*, to become spinners. Mayflies mate over the water, often in swarms. Females deposit their eggs by spinning just above the surface and repeatedly dropping to the water. *Spent* mayflies, like this Trico Spinner imitation (inset), have wings that lie flat on the surface.

OTHER AQUATIC FOODS and their imitations include: amphibians, such as a (1) frog, imitated by (2) Krazy Kicker Frog; terrestrials, such as a (3) grasshopper, imitated by (4) Dave's Hopper; aquatic insects, such as a (5) stonefly nymph, imitated by (6) Black Stonefly, (7) caddisfly larva, imitated by (8) Peeking Caddis, (9) midge larva, imitated by (10) Brassie; crustaceans, such as a (11) scud, imitated by (12) Olive Scud, and a (13) crayfish, imitated by (14) Dave's Crayfish. Larger fish, particularly brown trout and smallmouth bass, feed on minnows and other baitfish, such as a (15) sculpin, imitated by (16) Muddler Minnow.

Fly-Tying Tools & Materials

Fly-Tying Tools

Learning to tie flies with the right tools can make the difference between success and frustration.

Although most flytiers eventually accumulate a sizable collection of tools for a variety of specialized tasks, the beginner need only be concerned with the following basic tools: a fly-tying vise; scissors; thread holder, or bobbin; hackle pliers and hair stacker. Other handy tools include a whip finisher, dubbing needle, tweezers and hackle gauge.

It's a good idea to try a number of different styles of each tool you plan to buy. Your local fly tackle dealer can help you choose equipment to fit your skills and budget.

The following pages are intended to acquaint you with just a few of the many different styles of quality tools available. Your final choice is a matter of personal preference.

Fly-tying Vises

A good fly-tying vise should be easy to use, hold the hook securely and adjust easily to a wide range of hook sizes.

For most flytiers, a simple lever-action vise is adequate. However, for large bass and pike patterns, many tiers prefer a spring-loaded vise, which adjusts automatically to almost any size hook.

Vises come in clamp and pedestal models. Clamp models attach securely to your tying surface; the C-clamp should fit tables up to 1½ inches thick. Pedestal models should be heavy enough to stay in one place as you tie. Because of their weight, however, they are somewhat less portable than clamp models.

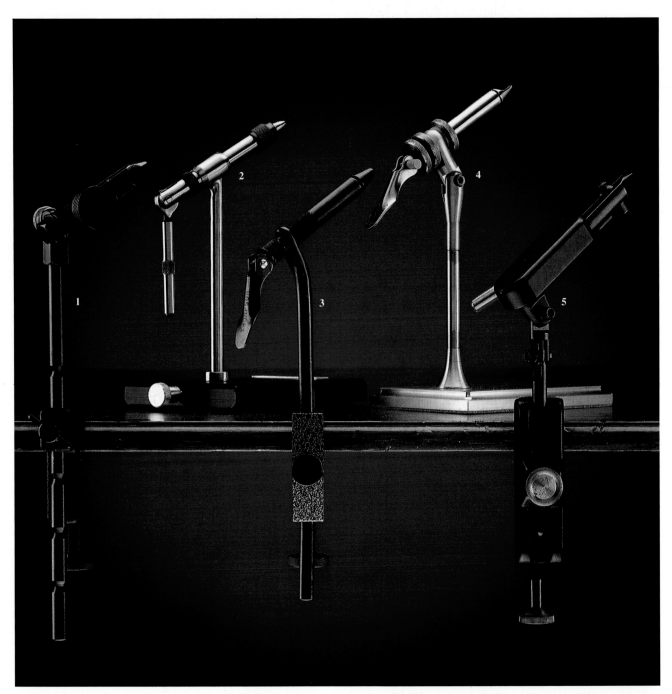

POPULAR VISES include: (1) Griffen clamp-base model with screw-adjustable head and jaws, for most fly-tying tasks; (2) Dyna-King Traveler, a pedestal model with rotary head, which allows for 360-degree viewing of fly; (3) Thompson Model "A," a fixed-head vise with lever-adjustable jaws and clamp base, for all-purpose tying; (4) Orvis Premier, a rotary-style vise with adjustable head angle, which allows you to tie materials to bottom of fly without removing hook; and (5) Regal spring-loaded model, which adjusts to a wide range of hook sizes.

Bobbins

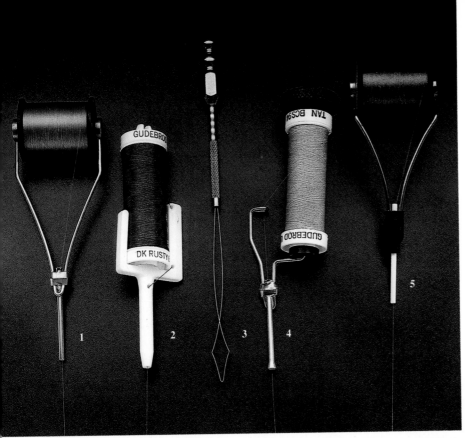

BOBBINS and accessories include: (1) traditional open-frame bobbin for standard-size spools; (2) vertical thread holder for long spools; (3) wire-loop tool for threading bobbin; (4) multi-spool bobbin, which fits a variety of spool sizes; and (5) bobbin with smooth ceramic tube, designed to reduce snagging or cutting of thread.

The bobbin performs several important functions. It holds the spool of thread as you tie, allows you to wrap the thread onto the hook precisely where you want it, and maintains proper tension on the thread. Whenever you pause to add or trim materials, simply let the bobbin hang below the hook. The weight of the bobbin keeps the fly from unraveling. You can add weight to your bobbin by inserting lead into the spool before attaching it to the bobbin.

The most popular style of bobbin is the open-frame. Choose a bobbin that fits comfortably in the palm of your hand.

Scissors

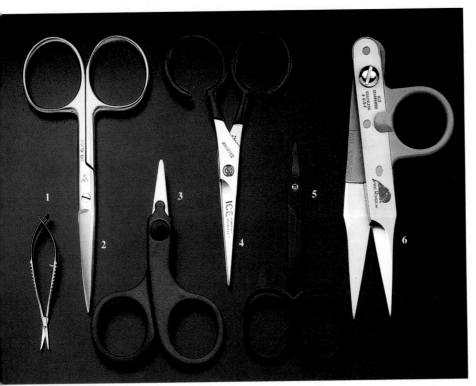

SCISSORS include: (1) surgical-style for delicate work; (2) serrated-blade for precision cutting; (3) ceramic-blade, which eliminates the need for sharpening; (4) fine-point and (5) curved-blade for close-in work; and (6) spring-type, excellent for palming.

The scissors you buy for fly tying should be very sharp and have a fine point for close-in work. Select models with stainless-steel or ceramic blades. Ceramics cost more but never need sharpening.

Many professional flytiers keep their scissors in the palm of their hand while they tie. It's a good habit to get into, and will save frustration and time otherwise spent looking for misplaced scissors. Spring-type scissors (left) are designed specifically for palming.

Sewing scissors work fine for flytiers with small hands, but most men find the finger holes too small.

Hackle Pliers

Hackle pliers simplify the job of winding hackle. Select a model that will grasp the hackle tip firmly without slipping. The jaws should not have any sharp edges that could cut the hackle.

If your hackle pliers are cutting too many hackle tips, dull the edges with a fine file or hook honer.

Hair Stackers

A hair stacker is an essential tool for aligning the tips of many types of fibers. To use a hair stacker, place the funnel into the stacker. Put a small clump of hair into the funnel, tips first, then tap the stacker firmly against a hard surface several times. Remove the funnel and grasp the tips of the hair fibers carefully. The tips should be perfectly aligned.

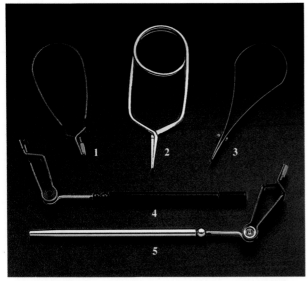

HACKLE-PLIER styles include: (1) duplex, with padded jaws; (2) traditional English; (3) teardrop, with fine-point jaws; (4) rotating, which reduce the chance of breaking hackle; and (5) rotating, with half-hitch tool at end of handle.

HAIR STACKERS include: (1) small stacker for small bundles of hair; (2) adjustable stacker for longer types of hair; and (3) magnum stacker for aligning larger bundles of hair when tying bass bugs.

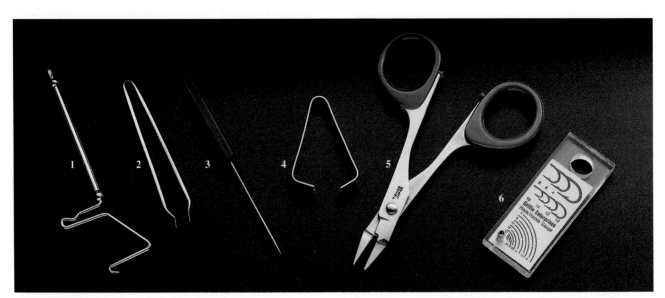

OTHER TOOLS include: (1) whip-finish tool for tying a secure finishing knot at head of fly; (2) tweezers for holding small materials, and other tasks; (3) bodkin, or dubbing needle, for combing out underfur, applying head cement and many other tasks; (4) hair packer for building dense spun-deer-hair bodies; (5) small pliers with flat jaws for safely mashing down hook barbs, when desired; and (6) hackle gauge for sizing hackle feathers.

Hooks

The hook is the foundation of any fly pattern. But the many different styles, shapes and sizes of hooks available can confuse the beginning flytier.

In most cases, however, the novice flytier need only be concerned with two hook styles: the dry-fly and wet-fly.

Hooks for dry flies are made with light-gauge wire to help them float on the surface. Wet-fly hooks, which include streamer and nymph hooks, are generally heavier, to help them sink quickly.

The size, length, wire and shape of a hook all determine how the finished pattern will look and behave on or in the water.

SIZE. The size of a hook is expressed by a number; the larger the number, the smaller the hook. For example, a #20 hook is smaller than a #10. Hooks larger than a size #1 are expressed as a number followed by a slash and a zero, such as "2/0." Hook sizes larger than 1/0 are in ascending numerical order; a size 5/0, for example, is larger than a 3/0.

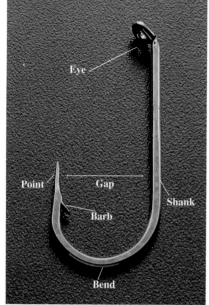
Parts of a hook

LENGTH. The length of a hook is expressed as standard, short or long. Any length other than standard is indicated by an "x." For example, a longer hook length may be described as "2x long"; shorter-than-standard, "2x short." The higher the x number, the longer or shorter the hook shank.

WIRE. The weight or gauge of the hook wire determines its suitability for a specific type of fly.

Hook weight other than standard is indicated by an "x." A slightly heavier-than-standard wire, for example, will be labeled as "1x heavy"; lighter, "1x light."

STYLES. Traditionally, hook style was indicated by names like "Limerick," "Sproat" and "Viking," which refer to the shape of the bend. Today, however, hook manufacturers are beginning to label hooks by function rather than style of bend. These include "caddis pupa," "streamer" and "flat-bodied nymph." Choose your hook depending on the type and size of fly you're tying.

HOOK EYES. Hooks come in three main eye types: turned-up eye (TUE), turned-down eye (TDE) or straight. Any one of these hooks will work for any fly; the choice depends on personal preference.

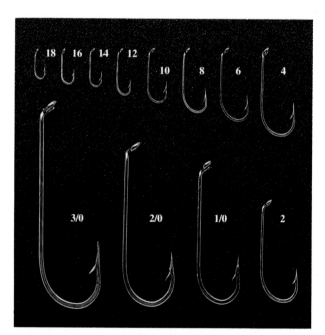

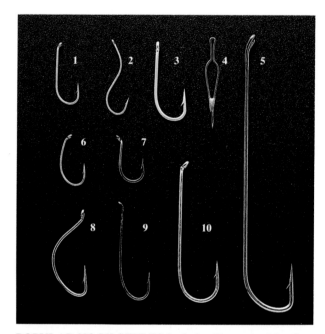

POPULAR HOOK SIZES for fly patterns range from size 18 to size 4. Larger hooks, from size 2 to 3/0, are used for specialty flies, including bass and salmon patterns. Hooks smaller than size 18 are used for tiny mayfly and midge imitations.

POPULAR HOOK STYLES include: (1) standard dry-fly, (2) swimming-nymph hook, (3) straight-eye; (4) flat-bodied nymph, (5) "Carrie Stevens" 10x long streamer; (6) caddis pupa; (7) 5X short with turned-up eye; (8) stinger nymph; and streamers with (9) turned-up and (10) turned-down eyes.

THREADS FOR FLY TYING include: (1) virtually unbreakable 1/0 Kevlar, (2) 3/0 Monocord, (3) fine-diameter 6/0 Fly Master, (4) extra-strong 3/0, (5) extra-fine 8/0. Apply additional wax to prewaxed thread (inset), if desired.

Thread

Fly-tying thread secures the materials onto the hook while adding as little bulk as possible. When choosing fly-tying thread, consider diameter, material and strength.

Antique 00, or 2/0, silk thread

Until recently, fly-tying thread was made of silk. And many flytiers still feel it is superior. But the majority of flytiers have turned to synthetic threads. Synthetics allow you to use finer-diameter threads without sacrificing strength; they come in a wider choice of colors, including fluorescents; and, unlike silk, are available prewaxed, which means they hold materials better than silk does. Some flytiers add wax to prewaxed thread for greater adhesion.

Recent innovations in thread include new materials, such as Kevlar and Spectra, that are virtually unbreakable. These threads are used for tying large bass patterns. Another innovation is extra-fine-diameter thread, for tying very small flies.

Historically, thread size, or diameter, was indicated by a series of zeroes. The more zeroes, the smaller the diameter of the thread. These zeroes are now abbreviated by a number followed by a zero; in other words, a 000 thread is labeled "3/0." A 3/0 thread has a larger diameter than a 6/0.

Common thread sizes range from 1/0, the largest, to 12/0, the smallest. Select the finest-diameter thread you can handle comfortably without breakage. Choose 3/0 to 12/0 for dry flies, wet flies and nymphs; 6/0 to 1/0 for streamers and bass patterns.

Materials

The endless array of feathers, fur and man-made materials can be intimidating to the beginning flytier. Before you stock up, it's a good idea to study the recipes for the flies you plan to tie and familiarize yourself with the materials you'll need.

Fly-tying materials are divided into the following categories:

FEATHERS. The most commonly used feathers for fly tying are:

Hackle feathers. The term hackle has two different meanings in fly tying. It is used to describe the collar of fibers near the head of a fly; but it also refers to the neck, back or tail feathers of a domestic or wild fowl. These feathers are used for tying tails, wings and, of course, hackle.

When selecting hackle feathers, don't be confused by names like grizzly and badger. They're not types of material, just distinctive colors. Grizzly hackle, for instance, has well-defined black-and-white

HACKLE FEATHERS come from: (1) rooster saddle-hackle capes, (2) rooster neck-hackle capes and (3) hen neck-hackle cape. Individual feather types (inset) include: (4) rooster neck hackle, (5) spade hackle from rooster neck, (6) rooster saddle hackle, and (7) hen neck hackle.

HACKLE CAPES supply various-size feathers. (1) Large feathers can be found at the top of the cape; (2) smaller ones, at the bottom.

barring; badger is cream colored with a dark brown stripe along the stem.

Following are the three basic types of hackle feathers:

• **Neck Hackle.** Rooster neck hackle is long and narrow with straight, stiff fibers and a bright sheen. It is perfect for hackling dry flies. Hen neck hackle is more rounded at the tips and is commonly used for dry-fly wings. Neck hackle is usually sold as a complete skin, or *cape*, in a variety of natural and dyed colors.

• **Saddle Hackle.** The larger feathers from the back of a rooster or hen are called *saddle* hackle. These feathers have more soft, absorbant material, called *webbing*, close to the stem. Hen saddle hackle is commonly used for wet-fly collars.

• **Spade Hackle.** On a rooster cape, the large feathers at the sides are called *spade* hackle. Spade hackle fibers are used most often for dry-fly tails.

Wing feathers. Fibers from a primary wing feather of a turkey, duck or goose are commonly used for wings on wet and dry flies. Segments cut from a matching pair of primary feathers are used for making *quill-segment* wings (p. 62).

The short fibers on the leading edge of a duck, goose or turkey primary wing feather are called *biots*. They are commonly used for tailing nymph patterns (p. 41).

Body, head and tail feathers. Body feathers come from the flank, breast or back of any game bird or domestic fowl. They are used primarily for winging dry, wet and salmon flies. Crest feathers come from the top of the head; tippets, from the neck.

Tail feathers usually come from large, exotic birds, such as ostrich and peacock. The long, green

COMMON TYPES OF PRIMARY FEATHERS include: (1) duck, (2) goose, and (3) turkey. These feathers come in a wide range of natural and dyed colors.

BODY AND HEAD FEATHERS include: (1) turkey flat, (2) partridge, (3) grouse, (4) jungle cock, (5) Lady Amherst pheasant tippet, (6) guinea, (7) golden pheasant crest, (8) golden pheasant tippet, (9) silver pheasant, (10) mallard flank, (11) wood duck flank, (12) teal flank and (13) cul-de-canard (CDC), from oil-gland area of a duck.

23

OTHER FEATHER types include: (1) peacock sword; (2) eyed peacock tail, source of peacock herl; (3) pheasant tail; (4) ostrich tail, source of ostrich herl; and (5) turkey marabou feather.

COMMON HAIR types include: (1) natural and (2) bleached Texas whitetail body, (3) dyed and (4) natural northern whitetail body; (5) moose mane; (6) bleached elk body; (7) dyed bucktail; (8) squirrel tail; and (9) calf, or kip, tail.

strands of the peacock tail feather, called *herl*, are used for body material in countless fly patterns.

HAIR. One of the most versatile fly-tying materials is animal hair. The natural variations in color, size, density, buoyancy and texture make this material an essential part of any flytier's inventory.

Hair is used mainly for tails, wings and bodies on dry-fly patterns. It can also be used on bass bugs.

Common hair types include deer, elk, moose, calf and squirrel.

FUR. Finer in texture than hair, fur is used to make *dubbing*, which is applied to the tying thread. The dubbed thread is then wrapped around the shank of the hook to form a body (p. 48). The term dubbing also refers to this method of body construction.

Different fur colors, both dyed and natural, can be blended to form dubbed bodies that closely resemble those of real insects.

When blended with synthetic fibers, such as Antron or polypropylene, natural fur dubbing gains durability and sparkle.

Long, stiff fur fibers, called *guard* hairs, are used for making nymph bodies and the tails of some flies.

WOOL, FLOSS AND CHENILLE. Wool may be the oldest fly-tying material and is still an ingredient in many fly patterns. Wool remains popular for nymph and wet-fly bodies because it is highly absorbent.

Flosses and chenilles, originally made of silk, are now more commonly made from synthetics, such as rayon and nylon, and are available in a wider range of colors.

OTHER SYNTHETICS. Synthetic materials are used not only for making bodies, but also for creating realistic wings, legs, tails and ribbing. Synthetics are more durable than natural materials, and add sparkle, flash and fluorescence to some patterns.

POPULAR FUR TYPES and the dubbing they produce include: (1) Hare's mask, which has both short fur for dubbing and guard hairs for making tails; (2) otter; (3) muskrat; (4) black goat; (5) beaver; (6) red fox.

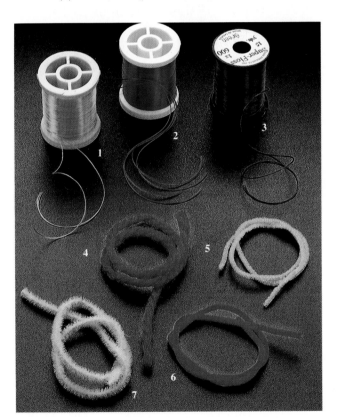

FLOSS, WOOL AND CHENILLE types include: synthetic floss in (1) two-strand, (2) four-strand and (3) single-strand; (4) wool yarn; synthetic chenille in (5) ultra-thin, (6) medium and (7) large diameter. See recipe catalogs for specific applications.

OTHER SYNTHETIC fly-tying materials include: (1) Flashabou, (2) Krystal Flash, (3) body foam, (4) Z-lon, (5) Rubber Legs, (6) polypropylene and (7) Antron yarns, (8) Swiss Straw, (9) Ultra Hair, (10) Mylar tinsel, (11) Lite-Brite, (12) Mylar body tubing, (13) V-rib and (14) Larva Lace ribbing. See recipe catalogs for specific applications.

ACCESSORIES to help organize your work space include: (1) incandescent, flexible-arm drafting lamp that can be clamped onto fly-tying bench; (2) multicompartment hardware cabinet with labeled drawers for organizing small tying tools and materials; (3) comfortable, height-adjustable secretary's chair that rolls, swivels and provides good back support; (4) 1-ft. by 2-ft. piece of green felt that can be spread out on fly-tying surface to prevent eyestrain and protect work surface from spills and scratches. Simply shake out felt and fold up for storage.

Organizing Your Work Space

A well-organized work space can make your fly tying easier and more efficient.

Set up a fly-tying bench in a corner of the basement or spare bedroom, if possible. A comfortable chair will save your back, and a bright drafting lamp will reduce eyestrain.

For traveling, pack a few essential fly-tying tools and materials in a small tackle box (opposite), so you'll have everything you need to tie up a pattern to match the hatch.

KEEP your hook boxes in a well-labeled multicompartment storage box. It won't take up much space in your tying area, and you won't have to hunt for the right hooks.

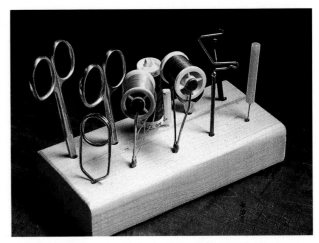

DRILL different-size holes in a small block of wood or Styrofoam® to keep your fly-tying tools organized and close at hand.

KEEP a small box of moist towelettes on your tying bench. Some commercially dyed materials leave a stain on your fingers; wiping them with a moist towel will keep you from spreading the dye to other materials.

SIZE and sort your hackle feathers ahead of time. Store your presorted hackles in a labeled, sealable plastic bag for easy access when you need them.

USE a Post-It® note to hold your sized hackle feathers, quill segments or other tying materials. The tacky surface holds the feathers safely and gently until you are ready to use them.

CARRY a tackle box when you travel to hold your vise, tools and materials essential for tying flies on the spot.

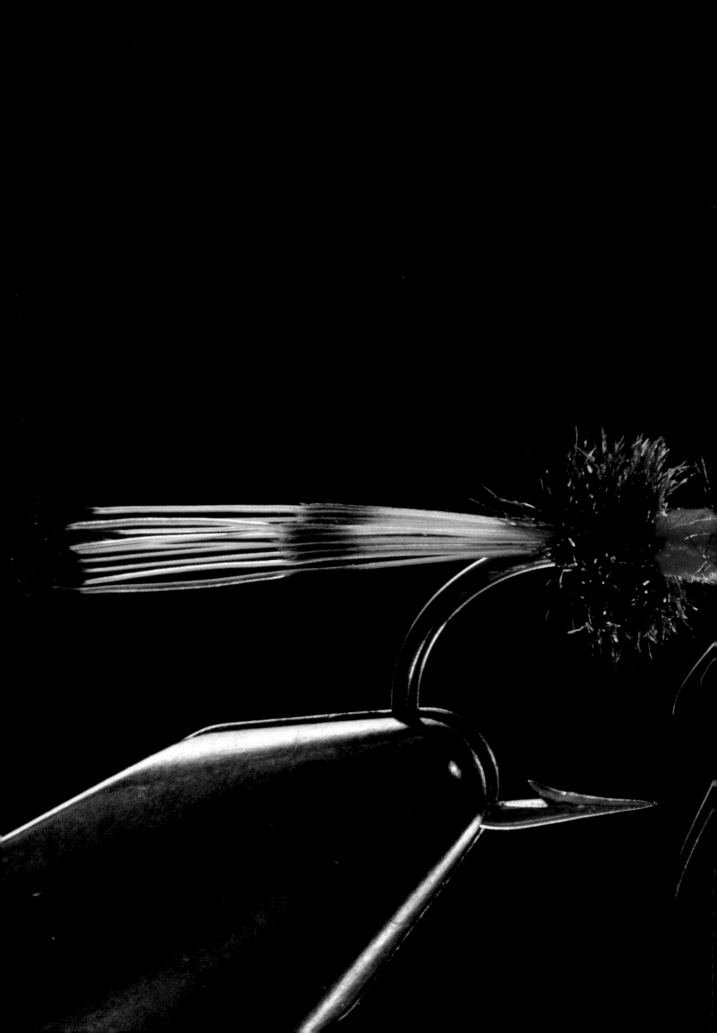

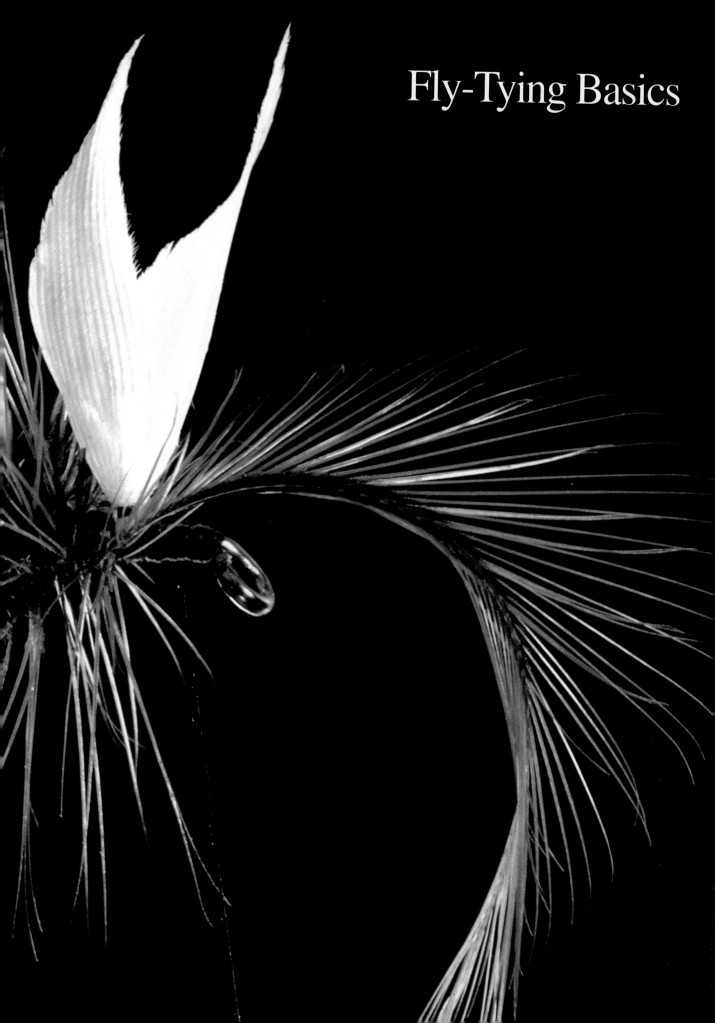

Fly-Tying Basics

Steps to Tying a Fly

DRY FLY

Tail · Body · Wing · Head · Hackle

NYMPH — Ribbing, Abdomen, Wingcase, Thorax

WET FLY — Tag, Beard

TERRESTRIAL — Legs, Underbody

STREAMER — Butt

BASS FLY — Collar

BASIC PARTS OF A FLY, shown on the dry fly (top), include tail, body, wing, hackle and head. Other parts found on some, but not all, flies include ribbing, abdomen, wingcase and thorax, shown on the nymph; beard or throat, and tag, shown on the wet fly; legs and underbody, shown on the terrestrial; butt, shown on the streamer; and collar, shown on the bass fly.

Once you are familiar with fly-tying tools and materials and you have a comfortable, well-lit workspace, you are ready to learn the basics of fly tying.

An artificial fly is made by winding one element after another — tail, body, wing, hackle and head — onto a hook. The secret to tying flies is understanding these elements and the techniques for combining them to create a complete fly.

This chapter is divided into eight sections (opposite), each covering a basic step in the fly-tying process. Often we'll show you different styles and techniques for completing each step.

Basic Fly-tying Terms

Fly tying has a language of its own. In this book, most of the terms are defined or explained the first time they appear in the text. But here are a few terms to keep in mind when getting started:

Tie-in point — the place on the hook where the thread was started or the last material was tied to the shank.

Forward or *ahead* — toward the eye of the hook.

Back or *backward* — toward the rear or bend of the hook.

1 GETTING STARTED. This section shows you how to put a hook in the vise, start the thread on the hook and control thread and materials (pp. 32 - 35).

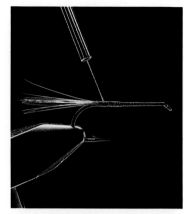

2 TAILS. The first ingredient in many fly patterns is the tail. In this section, you'll learn how to tie in several types of tails including hackle-fiber, hair, marabou and biot (pp. 36 - 41).

3 WEIGHTING THE HOOK. A good way to sink a nymph or streamer is to add weight to the hook before you tie in the body. This section shows you how to wrap lead wire around the shank or add a bead head to the hook (pp. 42 - 43).

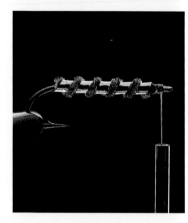

4 RIBBING. This section shows you how to give any fly a segmented appearance by wrapping the body with materials such as floss, tinsel or wire (pp. 44 - 45).

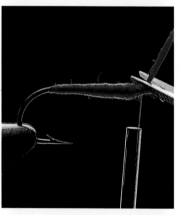

5 BODIES. In this section you'll see how to tie bodies of dubbing, floss, herl, quill and deer hair (pp. 46 - 55).

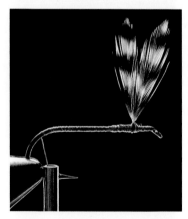

6 WINGS. This section shows you how to tie a number of different wing types including upright-and-divided, caddis- or down-wing, tent-style and parachute-style (pp. 56 - 65).

7 HACKLE. Hackle can be used to imitate legs, fluttering wings or even gills. This section shows you how to choose, prepare and wrap dry-fly, wet-fly, palmered and parachute-style hackle (pp. 66 - 71).

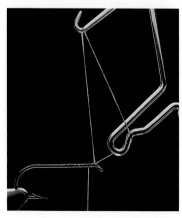

8 FINISHING KNOTS. When all the elements of a fly pattern have been wrapped onto the hook, it's important to finish your fly with a secure knot. You'll learn how to tie a half-hitch and use a whip-finish tool (pp. 72 - 73).

Getting Started

The first step in tying a fly is setting the head of the vise at a 30- to 45-degree angle and placing the hook so the shank is horizontal.

The jaws of the vise should grasp the hook at the lower part of the bend (right), not at the point. Many beginning flytiers try to hide the hook point in the jaws to avoid catching a finger or cutting the thread. Not only does this increase the chance of thread tension breaking the hook, but the jaws cover the gap, which is used as a gauge for measuring some tying materials.

If you plan to mash down the barb of the hook, do it before you begin tying; if your hook breaks in the process, you won't lose a finished fly.

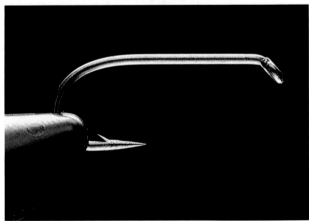

PLACE lower part of hook bend in jaws of vise, as shown. Tighten jaws just enough to hold hook securely without slippage; too much pressure can break hook. Spring-loaded vises adjust pressure automatically to hold most any size hook.

How to Start the Thread on the Hook

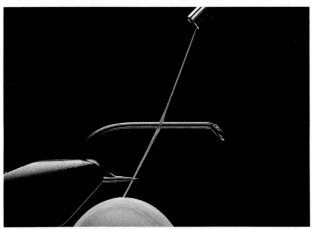

1 Place thread over hook at center of shank, as shown, with bobbin in your right hand and loose end of thread held firmly between left thumb and index finger.

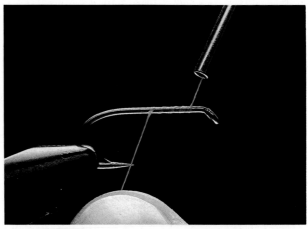

2 Make several thread wraps forward toward eye of hook, keeping tension on the thread with both hands. Always wrap away from you over top of hook.

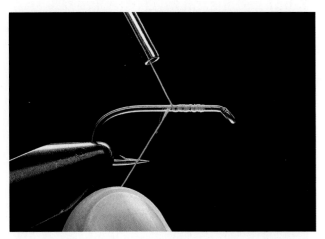

3 Wind thread back over first wraps. Practice keeping steady thread tension as you tie. Too much tension will break the thread, too little will allow materials to slip.

4 Trim off tag end of thread after it is secured by over-wraps. Keep tension on thread by letting bobbin hang below the hook.

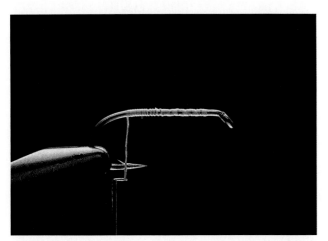

5 For patterns that require tying in the tail first, continue wrapping thread back to about $\frac{1}{16}$ inch from the start of the bend. Tie in the tail at this point. When wrapping near hook bend, angle thread away from hook point to avoid nicking or fraying the thread.

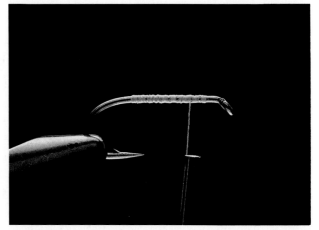

6 For patterns that require tying in the wings first, wrap thread forward again to about one-quarter hook-shank length from eye. Tie in the wings at this point.

Controlling Thread and Materials

When materials are wrapped with thread, they tend to shift and spread around the shank of the hook. The problem is caused by the pressure of the thread against the materials.

One way to prevent this is to use the *soft-loop*, or *pinch*, method. Another is to use the *controlled-slide* method, which lets thread tension work for you. Both methods will save you time and frustration later on.

1 Hold materials between thumb and forefinger and position materials on hook shank. Raise bobbin above hook so thread is taut against near side of materials.

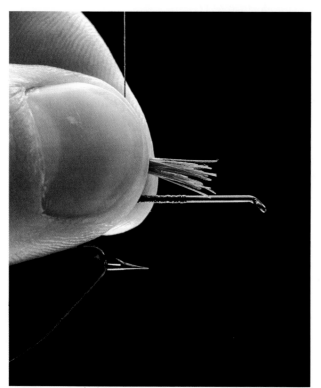

2 Pinch thread between thumb and forefinger to keep tension on thread and hold materials in place.

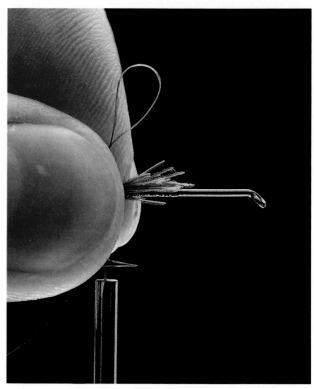

3 Form a slack, or soft, loop above materials. Bring thread back down other side of materials, and slide thread between thumb and forefinger without releasing the tension.

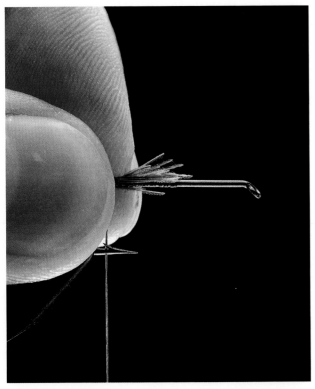

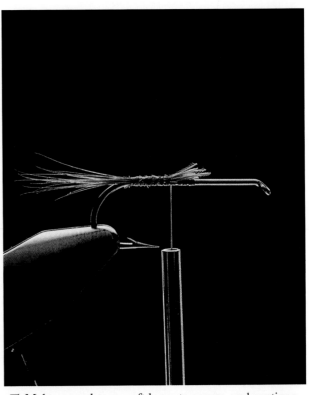

4 Slowly pull bobbin straight down, keeping pressure on thread and materials with thumb and forefinger.

5 Make several more soft loops to secure, and continue wrapping.

The Controlled-slide Method

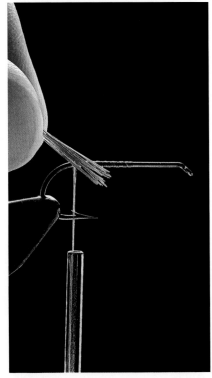

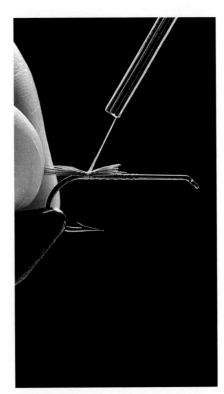

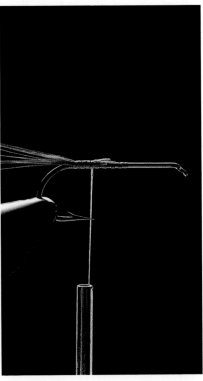

1 Position materials beside the hook shank at a slight angle as shown, to prevent them from spreading as you make first wrap.

2 Wrap thread over materials and around hook shank several times. Thread tension should slide materials onto top of hook.

3 Continue to wrap forward over materials to secure. Practice until you get a feel for the proper angle and thread tension.

Tails

TAIL types include: (1) marabou, as shown on this Woolly Bugger streamer; (2) hackle-fiber, as on this Light Cahill dry fly; (3) biot, used to make the distinct forked tail on this Prince nymph; and (4) hair, shown on this Grizzly Wulff dry.

Most artificial flies just don't look right without a tail; after all, the majority of the naturals you're imitating have a tail of some type.

Whether it's the delicate hackle fibers of a tiny mayfly imitation, or the bushy clump of marabou on a large streamer, the tail of an artificial fly serves several purposes.

On a dry fly, for example, a few fibers tied in at the bend of the hook add realism and help support the fly on the surface of the water. On a subsurface pattern, downy feathers add a lifelike swimming action.

COMMON TAIL TYPES. Following are the four most widely used types of tails:

Hackle-fiber. Catskill flytiers of the early 1900s introduced dozens of delicate dry-fly patterns, with sparse tails made from the fine, straight fibers of a hackle feather.

Tails of this type are now the most common, not only on dry flies, but also on wet flies and nymphs. Hackle-fiber tails are made from rooster or hen hackle and resemble a natural insect tail. Other materials can be tied in as you would hackle fibers to create tails with a slightly different look.

Wood duck flank fibers, for instance, give the tail a barred effect. Lady Amherst pheasant tippet gives it a black-and-white coloration; golden pheasant, a striking gold-and-black.

Pheasant tail fibers, used mainly for nymphs, are thicker than hackle fibers, so they can be tied in to mimic individual tail filaments.

Hair. The late Lee Wulff popularized the use of animal hair, particularly deer and calf hair, in his very successful "Wulff"-style flies. These patterns are tied with bushy hair tails and wings, and were originally designed to withstand swift western rivers and huge Labrador brook trout.

Today, hair tails are used on many dry-fly patterns. Tails made from moose, calf and deer-body hair float well and are especially durable. Subsurface patterns often have tails made from rabbit-hide strips or squirrel tail to give them more action.

Marabou. Marabou tails seem to breathe and pulsate under water, giving almost any pattern a lifelike appearance. These downy feathers from the leg of a turkey are dyed in a wide range of colors, and are used for tailing streamers, nymphs and bass flies.

Pulsating tails can also be made from hen saddle-hackle feathers and the short strands of herl from a peacock sword feather (p. 24). These tails are tied in as you would marabou tails.

Biot. Tails made from biot fibers closely resemble the two splayed tail filaments of a natural stonefly nymph. But biots can also be used as a substitute for a hackle-fiber tail on many other nymphs and wet flies.

The pointed biot fibers come from the leading edge of a primary wing feather. The most popular sources are goose and duck, although pheasant and turkey biots also are used.

Many flies, particularly bass bugs and streamers, are tied with tails made from synthetic materials (p. 24), and you can substitute synthetics for natural materials in most patterns. Synthetics are generally more durable, flashy and colorful than natural fibers.

Tips for Tying Tails

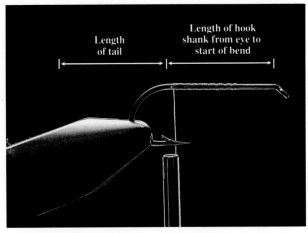

MEASURE tail fibers against hook shank. As a rule, length of tail on dry and wet flies should equal length of shank from hook eye to start of bend. Biot tails on nymphs are measured against hook gap (p. 41).

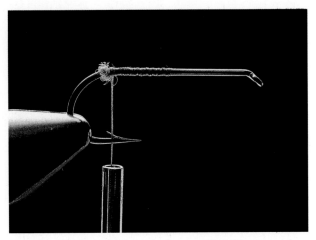

MAKE a tail that slants upward or a split tail by wrapping a small amount of dubbing (p. 47) onto hook shank at bend before tying in tail fibers.

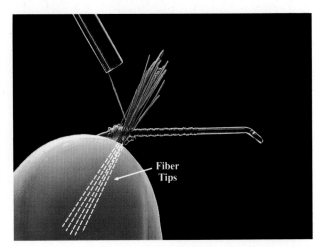

FAN tail fibers for more stability. Hold tips of fibers as shown (dotted line) and wrap with thread; fibers will spread horizontally, as on Grizzly Wulff (opposite).

Ginger-colored hackle fibers form the tail of this Ginger Fox dry fly

Hackle-fiber Tails

You can make hackle-fiber tails from any type of hackle. But spade-hackle fibers are best, because they are straight and stiff with very little webbing.

How to Tie In a Hackle-fiber Tail

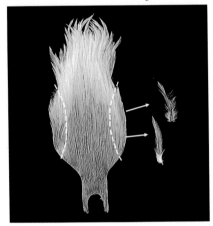

1 Select spade-hackle feathers from rooster neck cape in areas shown (dotted lines).

2 Pull a dozen or so fibers from stem. Grasp tips of fibers with your left hand and pull at 90-degree angle to keep tips aligned.

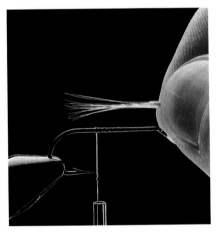

3 Size hackle fibers so they are slightly longer than hook shank. Tail should be same length as hook shank when tied in.

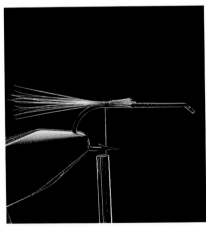

4 Position fibers on top of shank at hook bend. Tie in fibers with several soft loops.

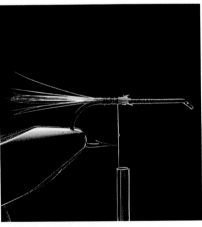

5 Make several thread wraps to secure fibers. Wrap forward to middle of shank. Tail should now lie directly on top of shank.

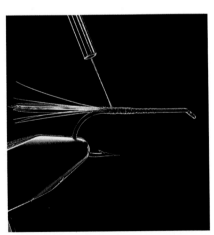

6 Wrap thread back to bend. You are now ready to tie in ribbing or body material.

Hair Tails

Beginning flytiers should practice making hair tails using calf or elk hair; deer hair tends to flare around the hook shank. You'll need a hair stacker for aligning the tips.

Calf hair is used to make the tail of this White Wulff dry fly

How to Tie In a Hair Tail

1 Snip a small clump of calf, elk or deer hair fibers.

2 Remove underfur by holding tips of fibers and combing a dubbing needle through butt ends.

3 Place fibers into funnel of adjustable hair stacker, tips first. Tap stacker sharply on surface several times to align tips. Too much hair will prevent proper alignment.

4 Remove funnel from stacker and carefully pull out fibers by the tips. Discard any short fibers.

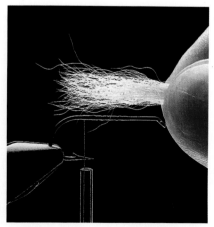

5 Measure fibers so tail will be same length as hook shank.

6 Tie in fibers at bend, using several soft loops. Use moderate thread pressure near bend to minimize flaring; increase tension as you wrap forward. Trim excess butts.

Marabou forms the tail of this Woolly Bugger

Marabou Tails

Marabou can be difficult to tie in because of the downy nature of the feather. But you can tame the fibers by stroking them with moistened fingers, as shown below.

How to Tie In a Marabou Tail

1 Select a marabou feather. Separate tip fibers from lower fibers.

2 Stroke marabou tips with moistened fingers to keep downy fibers under control.

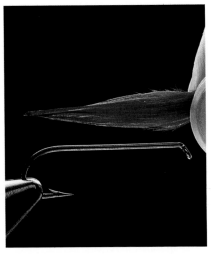

3 Measure marabou tip so tail will be same length as hook shank.

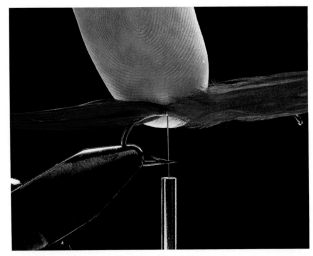

4 Tie in marabou feather on top of hook shank at bend, tips facing back, with several soft loops.

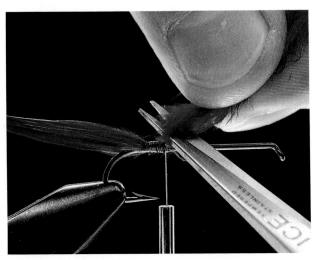

5 Wind thread forward over stem to secure. Trim off excess stem.

Biot Tails

Biot tails are generally shorter than other types of tails and are tied in with a different technique. A mound of thread at the hook bend helps make the biots flare.

Biot fibers form the tail and antennae of this Giant Black Stonefly Nymph

How to Tie In a Biot Tail

1 Snip two goose biots after bending stem. Set biots aside.

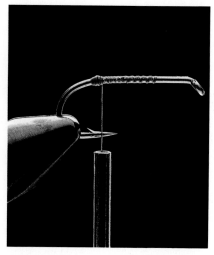

2 Start thread at midpoint of hook. Wind back to bend and form a small mound of thread.

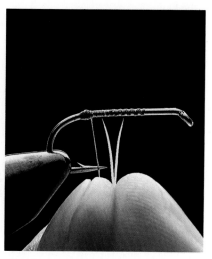

3 Measure biot against hook; tail length should equal hook gap.

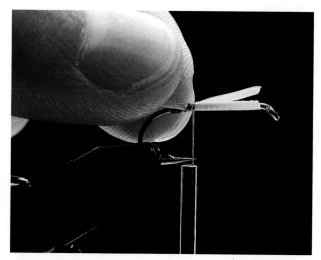

4 Place both biots in tail position, one on each side of hook, tips facing back. Secure butts with several soft loops just ahead of thread mound.

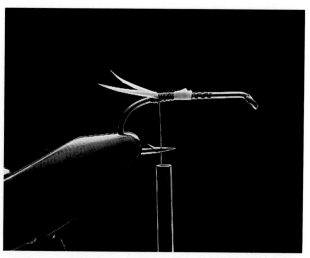

5 Wind thread back to middle of mound; this will make biot tips flare outward. Trim excess butts of biots.

Weighting the Hook

Streamer and nymph patterns are often more effective when fished deep. Many fly anglers just pinch a split shot onto their leaders. But split shot can weaken a delicate leader, interfere with your casting or simply fall off.

The best way to get the fly down in the current is to add weight to the hook before tying the fly.

You can weight the hook by wrapping the shank with lead or a substitute, or adding a drilled metal bead as a head.

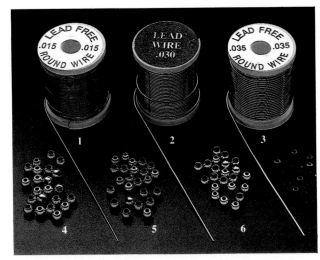

PATTERNS that can be tied with lead wire, or a substitute, include: (1) Pass Lake and (2) Peacock Caddis. Patterns with metal bead heads include: (3) Giant Black Stonefly, (4) Bottle Brush, (5) Thunderhead and (6) Pete's Pheasant Caddis.

MATERIALS for weighting hooks include: (1) light-gauge wire made from nontoxic lead substitute; (2) lead wire; (3) heavy-gauge lead-wire substitute; and metal beads in (4) brass, (5) copper, (6) nickel and (7) black finishes.

How to Wrap a Hook with Lead

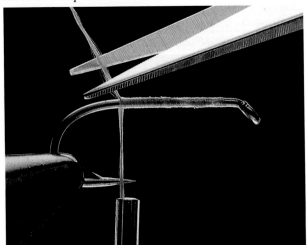

1 Wind thread onto a nymph or streamer hook; wrap back to hook bend, and trim tag end.

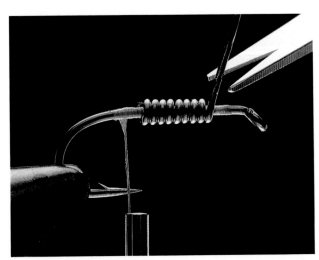

2 Wrap a length of fine lead wire, or substitute, onto hook in middle of shank. Trim excess wire.

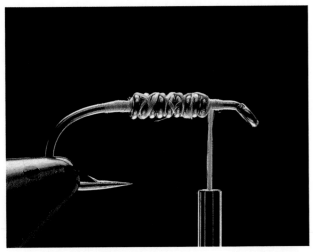

3 Wind thread forward and back over wire in open spirals, leaving a little space between each turn. Make several thread turns in front of wire to secure.

4 Continue wrapping until wire is just covered with layer of thread. Apply a coat of head cement, if desired. Continue tying pattern.

How to Add a Bead Head

1 Place nymph or streamer hook in vise. Mash down barb with small pliers to allow bead to slide over barb.

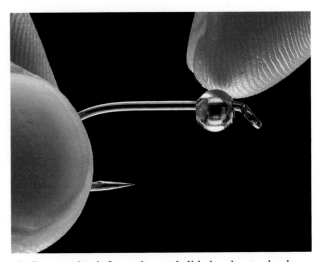

2 Remove hook from vise, and slide bead onto shank. Bead should rest against hook eye.

3 Replace hook in vise, wrap thread onto hook at midpoint of shank and trim tag end.

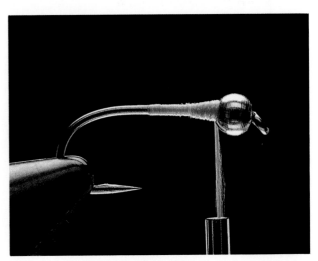

4 Wind thread forward and build a small mound of thread to hold bead in place. Continue tying pattern.

Tinsel ribbing adds flash, durability and a realistic, segmented appearance to this (1) Llama wet fly, (2) March Brown dry fly and (3) Gold-ribbed Hare's Ear soft-hackle fly

Ribbing

Many aquatic insects have segmented bodies. A few wraps of ribbing give the body a segmented look while adding durability and flash to most any fly pattern.

Experiment with various styles and colors of ribbing, even if the fly recipe doesn't call for it.

Flies with bodies made of biot or stripped quill (p. 52) appear segmented without additional ribbing material.

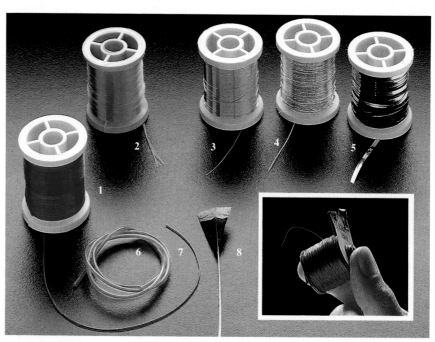

RIBBING MATERIALS include: (1) thread, (2) floss, (3) fine gold oval tinsel, (4) medium silver oval tinsel, (5) Mylar flat tinsel, (6) V-rib, (7) Larva Lace and (8) stripped grouse tail. Small motors (inset) are a good source for copper-wire ribbing.

How to Add Ribbing

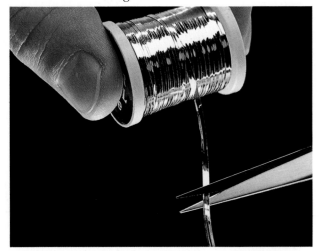

1 Cut a 3-inch length of ribbing material; allow enough material for tying in, wrapping and tying off. Ribbing material should be tied in *before* adding body material.

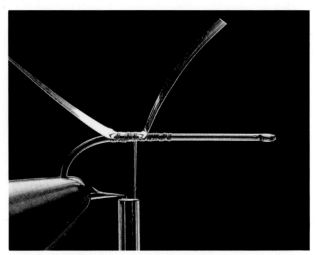

2 Tie in ribbing material on top of hook shank. Leave a tag end about ½ inch long. Make several thread wraps to secure.

3 Loop tag end of ribbing material back over itself, and secure with several turns of thread. Trim tag.

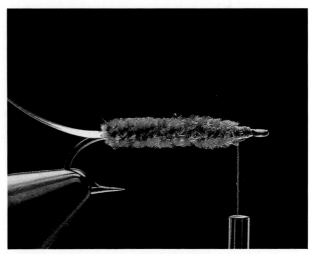

4 Add body material, such as chenille.

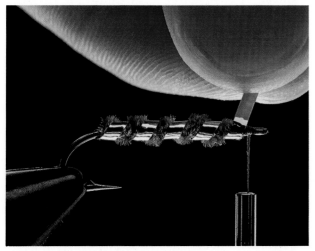

5 Wind ribbing forward over body material with four to six evenly spaced open-spiral wraps.

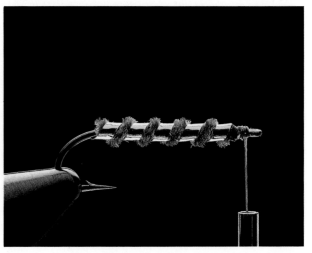

6 Secure ribbing with several turns of thread; trim excess ribbing material. Continue tying pattern.

Bodies

BODY styles include: (1) floss, in Tellico nymph; (2) spun deer hair, in Goddard Caddis dry fly; (3) quill, in Borcher Special dry; (4) dubbed, in Light Cahill dry and (5) Gold-bead Possie nymph; (6) herl, in Peacock Caddis dry.

Most flies have a simple body made of one or two elements; others, including many streamers, nymphs and wet flies, have very complex bodies.

BODY ELEMENTS. Following are the most common body elements, and definitions of each:

Wingcase — The protrusions on top of many nymph patterns, representing undeveloped wings.

Abdomen — The long, usually thin, part of the fly that begins just behind the wings or wingcase.

Thorax — The shorter, thicker section near the front of the fly.

Tag — A few turns of contrasting-color thread, floss or tinsel at or near the hook bend.

Butt — Several turns of material, such as herl, at the bend of hook; usually thicker than the tag.

Head —Made with extra thread wraps, by leaving butt ends of wing fibers exposed and trimming them, or by clipping spun deer hair to the desired shape.

Eyes — Sometimes added to patterns for more realism. The most common types are:

- Doll eyes. Available at most fly and hobby shops, these eyes are attached to the finished fly with waterproof glue.

- Painted. You can form eyes with dabs of acrylic paint (p. 77).

- Monofilament. Tie in a short length of heavy mono across the hook shank and lightly burn the ends to form eyes.

- Bead-chain. A length of standard bead chain will make several pairs of eyes. Snip a two-bead section and tie it in across the shank.

- Hourglass. Available in many sizes and colors, these eyes are attached by tying the neck across the shank.

BODY STYLES. Body styles of artificial flies range from the highly realistic to the fanciful. How a fly looks on or in the water depends on the materials and techniques you use to create the body. The five basic fly body styles include:

Dubbed. The most common type of body material, dubbing can be used to produce a variety of body shapes and thicknesses for almost all types of flies. Materials for dubbed bodies range from beaver and rabbit to synthetics, such as Antron.

Floss, wool and chenille. Available in both silks and synthetics, floss is used to form a fine, smooth body profile. It is also used to form a base layer, or *underbody,* that is wrapped with body material of contrasting color or texture.

Wool yarn, a traditional body material, forms a slightly thicker profile than floss.

Chenille is a yarnlike material, either silk or synthetic, which has a fuzzy texture that gives subsurface flies a pulsating action. Thin chenille is popular for small nymph bodies; thicker chenille, for bulky nymphs, streamers and bass bugs.

Herl. Herl is used mainly for dry flies, wet flies and nymphs, but many fly fishermen believe that it increases the effectiveness of any fly. This material, most commonly from the large tailfeather of a peacock, has a natural sheen that appeals to trout. Like wool yarn and chenille, herl is wrapped around the shank of the hook to form a bulky body.

You can form a thinner herl-style body by wrapping the hook with fibers from the tail or wing of other birds, such as pheasant or duck.

Quill. Although the term "quill" commonly refers to the stem of a large feather, in fly tying, it describes a fly body style. Quill bodies simulate the shiny, segmented look of a natural mayfly and are used on many dry- and wet-fly patterns.

The traditional source of quill is peacock herl with the fibers removed to expose the stem. Stripped hackle stems, biot fibers and grouse tail are substitutes for herl. Moose mane has black-and-white fibers that also make an excellent quill-like body.

Spun deer hair. The hollow fibers of deer-body hair make it unbeatable for tying bass bugs. The technique of allowing deer-hair fibers to flare around the shank of the hook is called *spinning.* Spun deer hair floats well and can be lightly trimmed to create a fat mouse- or froglike appearance for bass and pike patterns, or tightly clipped to form a dry-fly body.

Tips for Making Bodies

TAPER dubbed mayfly bodies slightly thicker at center of shank than at tail to mimic the natural.

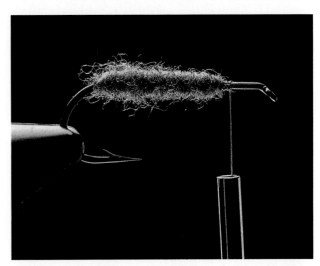

TAPER dubbed caddis bodies slightly thicker at tail than at head so wing lies flush over body.

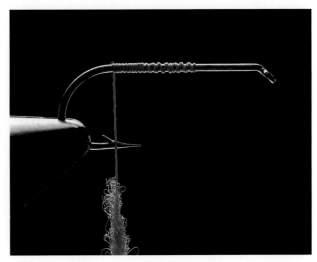

CHOOSE a thread color that matches the color of the body material to make the thread less visible.

This Damselfly nymph has a heavily dubbed body

Dubbed Bodies

As a rule, the dubbing on dry-fly bodies is thinner than that on wet flies or nymphs. This way, dry flies are light enough to float high, and their slim profile looks like that of an adult aquatic insect. To accomplish this, use a fine fur dubbing material, such as beaver, rabbit or muskrat.

Nymphs are usually dubbed to look fatter by adding more dubbing material to the thread and using thicker fur, such as fox, goat or the guard hair of hare's mask.

Synthetic fibers, or a combination of natural and synthetic, are also used for dubbing. Synthetics, however, can be tricky for the beginning flytier to control, because the fibers are longer and stretchier than fur.

You can add ribbing material to dubbed bodies to give the fly a segmented look.

How to Dub a Dry Fly, Mayfly Style

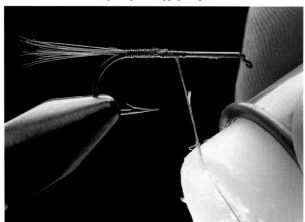

1 Apply a small amount of fly-tying wax to thread, if desired. Although most fly-tying thread is prewaxed, adding more wax to thread or to your fingers will help you form a tightly dubbed body.

2 Remove a small pinch of dubbing material, about the size of a dime, from package.

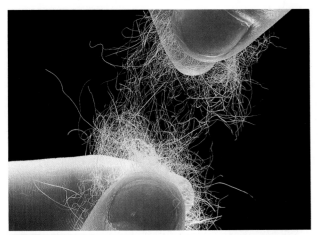

3 Separate fibers of dubbing material to eliminate any clumps.

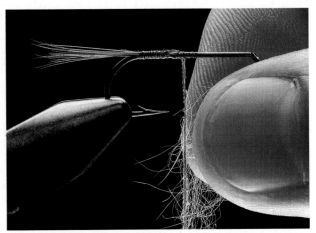

4 Apply a few fibers at a time to thread. Spin fibers firmly onto thread between your thumb and forefinger. Spin fibers in one direction only, or you will rub them off with every other spin.

5 Apply dubbing to three inches of thread. First inch should be only slightly thicker than thread itself. Add more dubbing below first inch until you see a slight increase in thread thickness.

6 Wrap dubbed thread back to hook bend, then reverse direction and wrap forward.

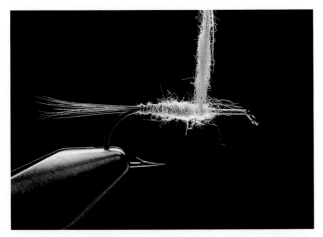

7 Continue wrapping dubbed thread forward around hook shank. The slightly thicker dubbing on last two inches of thread forms a tapered body.

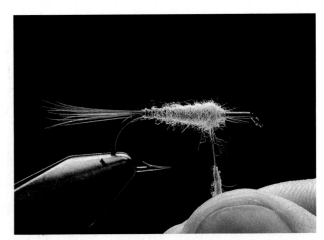

8 Wind dubbed thread forward to about midpoint of shank. Pull any remaining dubbing from the thread so you can continue to wind on materials.

Floss, Wool and Chenille Bodies

Most floss bodies are tied with multistrand material, but for small or delicate flies, all you need is a single strand of floss.

Wool and chenille bodies are tied in much the same way as the floss body below.

Yellow floss forms the body of this Caterpillar terrestrial pattern

How to Form a Floss Body

1 Cut an 8-inch length of multistrand floss.

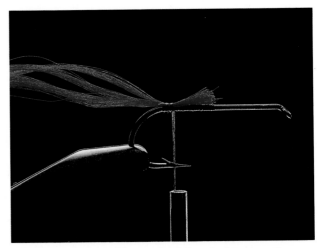

2 Tie in strands of floss at hook bend with several turns of thread. Wind thread forward over tag ends of floss to ⅛ inch behind eye.

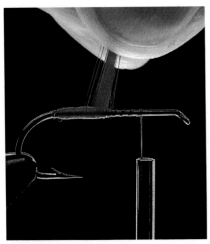

3 Grasp ends of strands; wrap floss forward around shank.

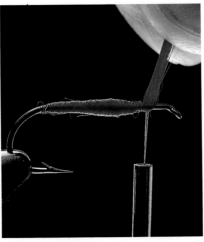

4 Form tapered body by slightly overlapping previous wraps as you wind forward.

5 Secure strands with several thread turns; trim excess floss.

Herl Bodies

Herl is commonly used as the main body material, but it also makes a good underbody, butt or palmered-style (p. 70) body wrapping.

Because herl is one of the most fragile body materials, many flytiers add ribbing for durability.

Peacock herl is used to tie this Theo's Danger Baby nymph

How to Tie a Herl Body

1 Snip two or three strands of herl from a large peacock tail feather.

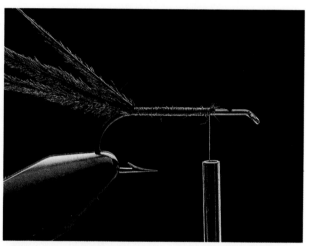

2 Tie in strands near hook bend with tips facing back. Secure strands with several turns of thread. Wrap thread forward over butt ends to a point one-third hook-shank length behind eye.

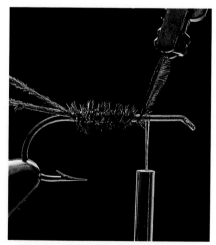

3 Grasp the tip of one strand of herl with hackle pliers. Wrap herl forward around hook shank, and secure.

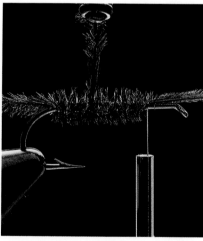

4 Grasp second strand with hackle pliers, wind forward and secure.

5 Wind third strand forward and secure. Trim ends of all strands and continue adding materials.

This classic Quill Gordon has a body of stripped peacock herl

Quill Bodies

One of the best materials for making quill bodies is herl from the tip of an eyed peacock feather. Herl strands from this part of the feather have stems with distinct light and dark edges, which give the body a striped appearance. Carefully strip the fibers from the stem using your fingers or a pencil eraser (below).

For a raised ribbing effect, make a quill body using biots (opposite).

How to Make a Quill Body from Stripped Peacock Herl

1 Pull a strand of peacock herl from an eyed peacock tail feather.

2 Place strand of herl on tying surface and carefully rub off fibers with eraser. Too much pressure may break the fragile stem.

3 Moisten stripped stem with water to reduce brittleness and prevent it from splitting as you wrap.

4 Tie in stem about one-third hook-shank length from bend. Wrap thread forward.

5 Wind stem back toward bend in an open spiral.

6 Reverse direction, and wrap stem forward in a tight spiral. Each wrap should touch previous wrap, to form smooth body profile.

7 Secure stem with several turns of thread. Trim excess stem.

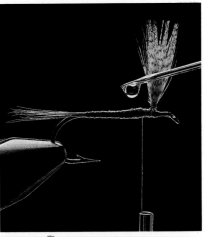

8 Apply thin coating of lacquer to quill body for durability.

How to Make a Quill Body from Biot

1 Snip one biot from stem with scissors.

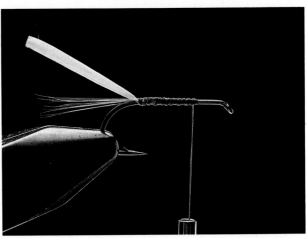

2 Tie in tip of biot at hook bend with several turns of thread. Wind thread forward as shown.

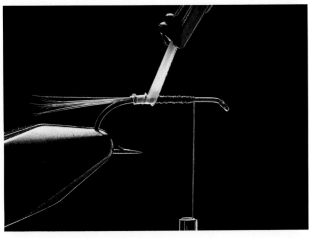

3 Grasp butt end of biot with hackle pliers and wrap forward around hook shank.

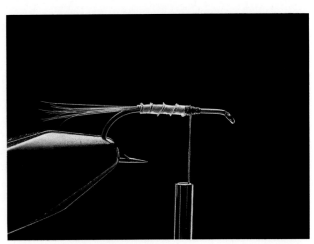

4 Secure biot with several turns of thread, and trim excess biot. Apply lacquer, if desired.

53

Several colors of dyed deer hair give this Deer-hair Bug its unique appearance

Spun Deer-hair Bodies

Spinning deer hair isn't difficult, but it takes some practice to learn and it's messy! Allow yourself plenty of time for mistakes and don't try it in the living room.

The trick to spinning deer hair is to use as much thread tension as possible without breaking the thread or bending the hook. Use a strong thread, such as Monocord or Kevlar. You'll want to use a hair packer (p. 19) to ensure a compact body.

Bass flies are tied with many deer-hair bundles, which are lightly trimmed to form bulky bodies. Dry flies require only a few small bundles, trimmed closely.

Deer hair comes dyed in practically every color. To create a multicolored body, alternate the color of the hair bundles you tie in along the shank.

How to Make a Spun Deer-hair Body

1 Clip a small bundle of deer hair from hide. Do not use too much hair at one time; the body of a bass bug is built of many small clumps tied in and packed.

2 Comb out the underfur with a dubbing needle, making sure all the downy fibers have been removed.

3 Snip off tips of deer hair, which are too fine to flare.

4 Hold deer hair by tips, and position bundle over hook shank at bend. Make several soft loops around middle of bundle to secure on top of shank.

5 Apply downward pressure on thread. Both ends of deer hair will begin to flare. Make several more thread turns through hair, keeping firm tension on thread.

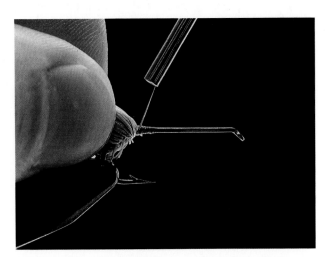

6 Draw fibers back with fingers, and make several thread wraps around shank in front of deer hair.

7 Push hair back toward bend with hair packer. This will make the body denser and easier to trim to the proper shape.

8 Add another small bundle of deer hair, repeating steps 3 through 7 until shank is filled. Leave room at hook eye, and whip-finish (p. 73).

9 Trim body to appropriate shape with scissors or razor blade.

WING styles and materials include: upright-and-divided, tied with (1) hair on White Wulff, (2) duck flank on Dark Hendrickson, (3) quill segment on Black Gnat, (4) hackle tips on Adams; caddis, tied with (5) hair on Elk Hair Caddis; down-wing, tied with (6) quill segment on March Brown; and parachute, tied with (7) hair on Light Cahill.

Wings

Wings imitate the profile of a natural insect. On dry flies, they also add visibility so the angler can better see the fly on the water, and they slow the fly's descent so it settles gently to the surface. On wet flies and streamer patterns, they add color or action.

A few strands of material of contrasting color are sometimes added to the top of the wing of a streamer or wet fly to form an *overwing* or *topping*, or beneath the wing to form an *underwing*. Contrasting materials tied to each side of the wing are simply called *sides*.

Cheeks, usually eyed jungle cock feathers, are also tied to the side of the wing of many wet-fly and streamer patterns.

When tying wings on any pattern, proportion is important (opposite). Wings that are too large can affect the balance of the fly, causing it to float on its side. Undersize wings will not produce the proper silhouette.

BASIC WING STYLES. Most fly wings fall into one of the following categories:

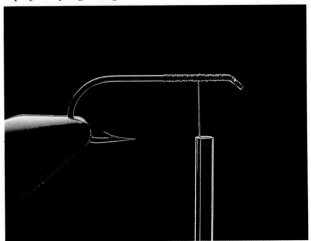

WRAP hook shank with thread to form a base for tying in the wings.

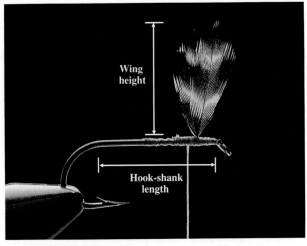

PROPORTION upright wing so it is equal in height to hook-shank length when tied in.

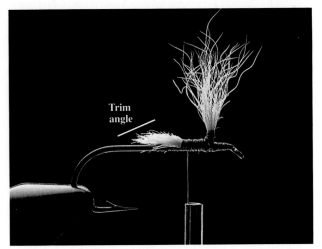

TRIM butt ends of wing material at an angle before over-wrapping with thread, for a tapered body.

CLIP a duck wing-quill segment 1½ times wider than the desired finished wing size. Segment will compress when tied in.

Upright-and-divided. Intended to imitate the wings of a natural mayfly or midge, upright-and-divided wings are the most common dry-fly wing style. The wings are tied in so they project at about a 45-degree angle from either side of vertical.

In a *spent-wing* pattern, a variation of the upright-and-divided style, the wings are tied to project at a 90-degree angle. This way, the wings rest on the surface, like the wings of a spent mayfly.

Spent wings are tied in just like upright-and-divided wings; simply cinch them down to the sides more to make them spread.

Caddis, Down-wing and Tent. These wing styles are tied in to lie flat or angle back over the body of the fly. They are used on wet flies, streamers and dry flies, particularly caddisfly and stonefly imitations.

Caddis and down-wing styles are similar, but caddis wings are shorter, resembling the mothlike wing of a caddisfly.

Tent-style wings are made with a folded quill segment, tied in over the back to mimic the folded wings of an adult insect.

Parachute. Used only on surface patterns, the parachute-style wing forms the base around which the hackle is wrapped horizontally. This wing-and-hackle combination causes the fly to settle slowly to the water, like a parachute, and ride low in the surface film.

These basic wing types can be tied with a variety of materials, each requiring a slightly different tying technique. Refer to pages 58 to 65 for instructions on tying the most popular wing styles.

A Hendrickson is tied with duck-flank wings, upright-and-divided

Duck-flank Wings, Upright-and-divided

The barring on these delicate feathers makes them the best imitation of a natural mayfly wing. When tied in, the wing has a natural mottled look and gives the illusion of fluttering.

Wood duck flank feathers are preferred for these wings, because of their distinct barring. But you can substitute teal or dyed mallard-flank feathers.

How to Tie In Duck-flank Wings, Upright-and-divided

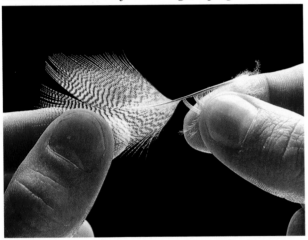

1 Select a large flank feather with a naturally squared-off end. Prepare feather by stripping away soft, downy fibers near base.

2 Fold feather lengthwise down the stem, with shiny side out.

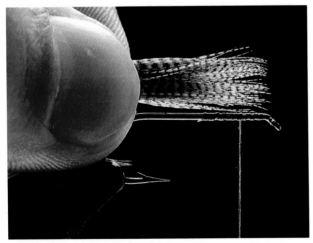

3 Measure folded feather so height of finished wing equals hook-shank length.

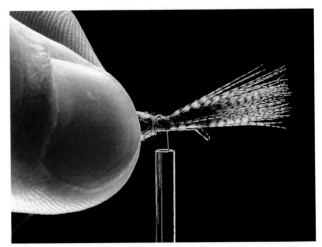

4 Position wing material over tie-in point, just ahead of midpoint of shank, tips facing forward. Tie in feathers, using several soft loops. Leave room between wing and hook eye for tying in hackle.

5 Wrap thread back toward bend to secure fibers. Trim off excess stem. Wind thread forward to tie-in point.

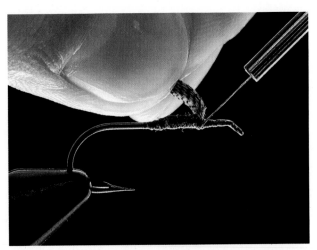

6 Set wings upright by grasping tips between thumb and forefinger. Make several turns of thread around hook shank in front of wings.

7 Divide fibers into two equal parts with dubbing needle or tips of scissors. Separate wings by gently pulling them to the sides.

8 Pass thread between wings from front to back, crossing over shank.

9 Bring thread around underside of hook and pass forward between wings, in a figure-eight pattern. Make a second figure eight.

10 Make one complete thread turn around base of far wing. Pass bobbin under shank, then make one complete turn around near wing.

11 Make several turns of thread around hook shank to secure wings. Wind thread back to hook bend, then add remaining materials.

This durable Royal Humpy has upright-and-divided hair wings

Hair Wings, Upright-and-divided

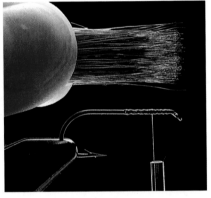

Hair wings are set upright-and-divided in much the same way as duck-flank wings. Usually made of deer, calf or elk hair, or a synthetic substitute, these wings are durable, buoyant and are easy for the fisherman to see on the surface of the water.

How to Tie In Hair Wings, Upright-and-divided

1 Snip a small bundle of hair from the hide. Comb out any underfur with a dubbing needle. Place hair in funnel of hair stacker, tips first.

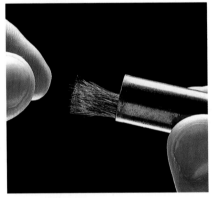

2 Tap stacker sharply against surface to align tips. Remove funnel from stacker, and pull fibers from bottom of funnel carefully by the tips.

3 Transfer butts to left hand, and measure fibers to proper length. Hair wings should be equal in height to shank length.

4 Tie in hair bundle, tips facing forward, on top of shank with several soft loops.

5 Trim off butt ends at an angle; wrap thread back over tapered cut to form a smooth foundation for the body material.

6 Set wings upright and divide as shown in steps 6 through 11 of duck-flank wings (p. 59).

Hair Wings, Caddis- and Down-wing Style

In caddis patterns, the mothlike wings are slightly shorter than the hook shank, when tied in. In down-wing patterns, the wings are equal to, or slightly longer than, the hook shank.

The wings on this Elk-hair Caddis are tied in over the body

How to Tie In Hair Wings, Caddis-style

1 Tie in body material. Leave about one hook-eye length gap behind eye; wrap the gap with thread to form base for wing.

2 Hold a small bundle of stacked hair by the butts; it should equal hook shank in length. Turn hair bundle around, and position over hook shank with tips facing toward hook bend.

3 Make one complete turn of thread around bundle of elk hair only, then make another around bundle and hook shank.

4 Cinch bundle on top of shank, and make several wraps to secure. Hair should not spin around shank. Whip-finish, and trim off thread.

5 Trim butt ends of elk hair at a slight angle to form a small, tapered head. Apply head cement to thread wraps for added durability.

The Black Gnat is tied with quill-segment wings, upright-and-divided

Quill-segment Wings, Upright-and-divided

For upright-and-divided wings, select a pair of matched quill feathers from opposite wings and tie them in before adding body material.

Quill segments may separate when you tie them in, but if you stroke the segments, the tiny barbules will lock the fibers together. Adding a drop of head cement to each segment before tying it in will reduce the chance of splitting.

How to Tie In Quill-segment Wings, Upright-and-divided

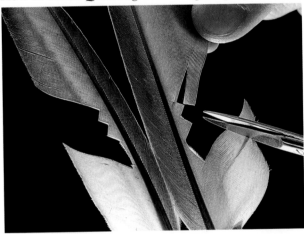

1 Select a matched pair of quill feathers from opposite wings. Snip a ¼-inch segment from the same place on each feather.

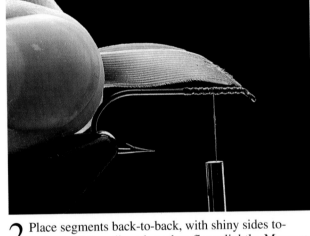

2 Place segments back-to-back, with shiny sides together and tips aligned, so they flare slightly. Measure segments to same length as hook shank.

3 Position segments over hook shank, curved side up, with tips facing forward. Tie in, using several soft loops. Trim butts, and secure ends with thread wraps.

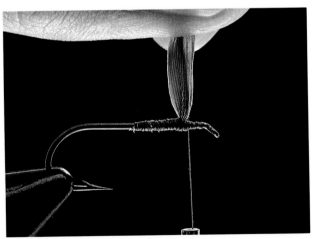

4 Set wings upright with several turns of thread around hook shank in front of wings.

Quill-segment Wings, Tent-style

For tent-style wings, tie in the body material first. Then select a single quill segment, fold it as shown below and tie it in.

You can also tie a two-segment, tent-style wing as on the Henryville Caddis (right). Simply tie in one folded segment on top of another segment of approximately the same size.

The Henryville Caddis is tied tent-style, using two quill segments

How to Tie In Quill-segment Wings, Tent-style

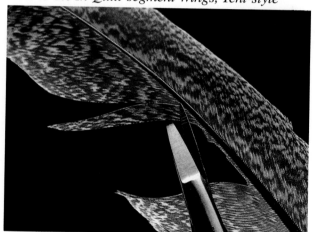

1 Snip one ¼-inch-wide segment from the wing quill feather. For a two-segment wing, select a matched pair of quills.

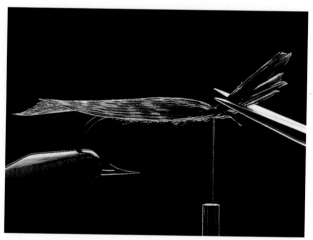

2 Position quill segment(s) over hook shank, tip facing back. Tie in with several soft loops, and trim butt end.

3 Gently fold quill segment(s) lengthwise along center to form tent shape.

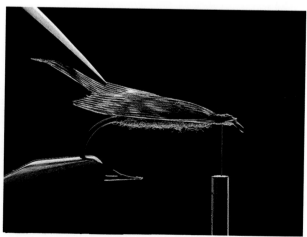

4 Cut tip of segment(s) to proper length, which is slightly longer than the hook itself. Cut each side at an angle to form a "V," if desired.

Hackle-point Wings, Upright-and-divided

Hackle-point wings are made from the tips, or points, of a hackle feather. They produce a realistic wing profile, but add very little weight to the finished fly.

Traditional hackle-point wings were made from rooster hackle. But the tips of modern rooster hackle are too narrow for the proper wing profile. As a result, flytiers now use the tips of hen neck hackle feathers, which are broader and more rounded.

This Mosquito pattern is tied with grizzly hackle-point wings

How to Tie In Hackle-point Wings

1 Select two medium-size hackle feathers. Align back-to-back so tips flare slightly.

2 Measure hackles; finished wing should equal hook shank in length. Trim hackle fibers from stem, leaving just the tips, or points, to form wings.

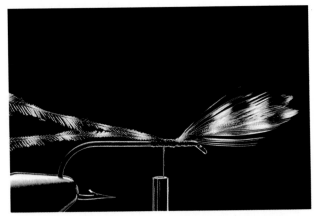

3 Position hackle points over hook shank, tips facing forward, and tie in with several soft loops.

4 Trim off stems, and set wings upright-and-divided (p. 59). Wrap thread back to hook bend, and continue tying pattern.

Parachute-style Wings

A parachute wing gives a dry fly a unique profile easily seen by fish and angler. The wing also serves as a base for wrapping the parachute-style, or horizontal, hackle (p. 71). This type of hackle causes the fly to float low in the surface film, much like an emerging mayfly.

Parachute wings can be made from many materials, including duck-flank fibers, hackle tips, calf tail and a variety of synthetic fibers. Use bright white or orange poly-yarn wing materials for extra visibility in low-light situations.

Parachute-style wing and hackle are seen in this Pink Lady pattern

How to Tie In a Parachute-style Wing

1 Select a small bundle of calf tail hair. Measure material so wing height equals hook-shank length.

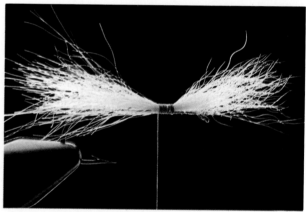

2 Tie in bundle with tips facing forward, as you would an upright-and-divided wing. Trim butt ends and wrap thread over them to form tapered base for body.

3 Set wing upright with several turns of thread around hook shank in front of wing.

4 Wrap thread horizontally around upright wing to form a ⅛-inch-high base for hackle. Add hackle as shown on page 71.

Hackle

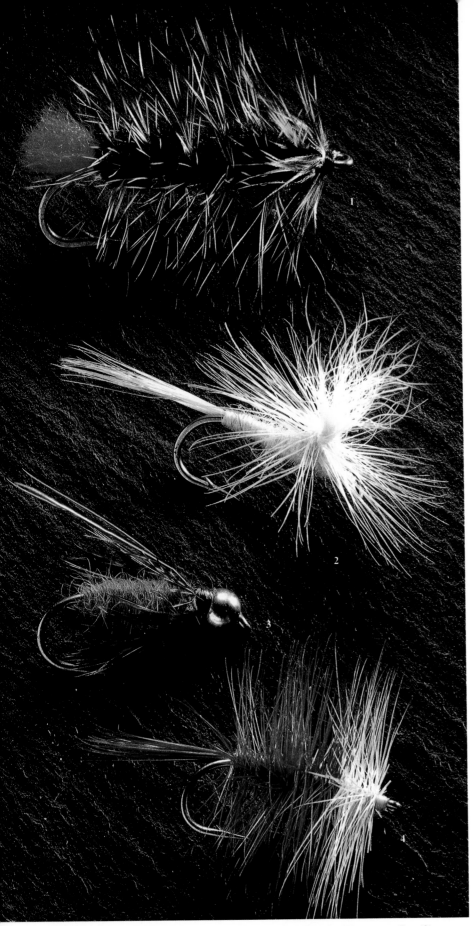

Hackle gives an artificial fly the illusion of life. It is used on most patterns to imitate legs, fluttering wings or pulsating gills.

Types of hackle include:

Dry-fly hackle — Made from the stiff, straight neck feathers of a rooster, this hackle forms the collar that gives a dry fly its characteristic profile and keeps it riding high on the water.

Wet-fly hackle — Used on both wet and soft-hackle flies, this type of hackle is made from hen-neck, saddle-hackle or partridge feathers, which are softer and more absorbant than dry-fly hackle.

Wet-fly hackle is first folded (right), so all the fibers are on one side of the stem and slant back over the body of the fly when tied in.

Wet-fly hackle is sometimes modified to form a *beard*, or *throat*, on the underside of the fly. With the top fibers trimmed away, the remaining fibers imitate the folded legs of an insect. You can also make a beard by tying fibers to the bottom of the hook shank.

Palmered hackle — Palmered hackle adds bulk without adding weight. Palmered rooster hackle makes dry flies float higher; hen hackle gives nymphs and wet flies lively action under water.

Parachute hackle — Parachute-style flies float lower in the water than standard dries. They rest in, not on, the surface, resembling natural emergers.

The effectiveness of parachute patterns leads many flytiers to experiment with this hackle on traditional fly patterns.

Choose stiff, straight rooster-neck hackle feathers, as you would for hackling dry flies.

HACKLE styles include: (1) palmered, as on this Wooly Worm wet fly; (2) parachute, as on this Light Cahill Parachute; (3) wet-fly, as on this Gold-ribbed Hare's Ear soft-hackle; and (4) dry-fly, as on this Brown Bivisible.

How to Measure Hackle

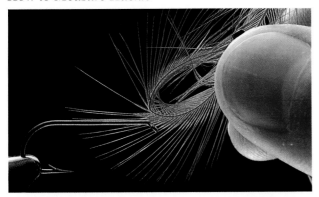

HOOK-LENGTH METHOD. Measure hackle against hook shank by bending feather as shown. As a rule, dry-fly, palmered and parachute-style hackle should be three-fourths hook-shank length, when tied in. Wet-fly hackle should equal length of shank. *Note:* never trim tips of hackle to achieve desired length.

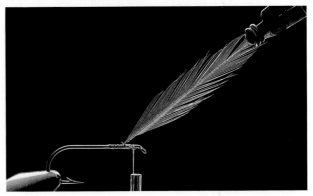

HACKLE-GAUGE METHOD. Use a hackle gauge to select the correct-size feather. Bend feather around post so tips cover lines on gauge. For dry-fly, palmered and parachute-style hackle, match fiber length to the size hook you are using, as indicated by numbers on gauge. Wet-fly hackle should be slightly longer for a given hook size.

How to Prepare Hackle

TRIM off soft, downy fibers, or webbing, near base of feather, leaving fiber stubs to help thread secure hackle. Snip off butt end, leaving approximately 1/4 inch of trimmed portion.

How to Use Hackle Pliers

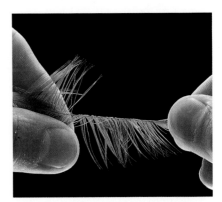

GRASP tip of feather with hackle pliers so stem and pliers are aligned. If you grasp feather crosswise, you are more likely to break off tip. Wind at a right angle to shank, using only enough pressure to keep hackle in place; too much will break tip of feather.

How to Fold Wet-fly Hackle

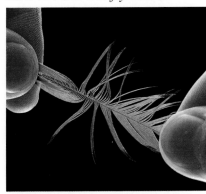

1 Select one large saddle-hackle, hen-neck hackle or partridge feather. Stroke all fibers back toward base of feather so they are at a right angle to stem.

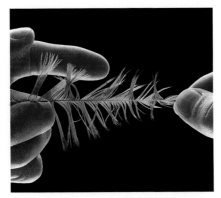

2 Grasp tip of feather, shiny side up, in right hand; hold base of feather in left hand as shown.

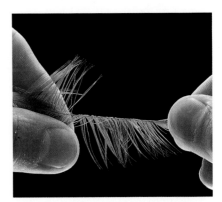

3 Stroke fibers downward between left thumb and forefinger until all fibers are folded to one side of stem.

Straight, stiff hackle fibers make up the hackle and body of this Brown Bivisible dry fly

Dry-fly Hackle

Dry-fly hackle is wound around the hook shank at wing position. The fibers radiate at a right angle to the shank to form the familiar collar.

On most dry flies, the hackle is about three-fourths the length of the hook shank.

How to Tie In Dry-fly Hackle

1 Select two rooster-neck hackle feathers of the proper size, and trim webbed portion. Align tips of feathers with shiny sides toward you. Place them alongside shank at base of wings, tips facing backward at a 30-degree angle.

2 Secure hackle stems with two turns of thread behind wing, then two in front. Trim any excess hackle stems.

3 Using hackle pliers, grasp the tip of the hackle farthest away from you. Pull hackle straight down below hook to begin winding.

4 Make several turns behind wing, then several in front. Wrap over hackle tip with thread to secure. Trim off hackle tip.

5 Grasp second hackle tip and weave it through first with a zig-zag motion to avoid crushing fibers of first hackle. Wrap thread over second tip to secure; trim tip.

Wet-fly Hackle

Wet-fly hackle must be folded before it is tied in (p. 67). This way the fibers angle backward, giving the fly a streamlined shape.

Wet-fly hackle should be slightly longer than dry-fly hackle, or about hook-shank length when tied in.

Black hen hackle fibers slope back over the body of this Hen-and-Brown soft-hackle fly

How to Tie In Wet-fly Hackle

1 Select and measure one large saddle hackle feather. Do not trim webbing; it absorbs water and helps sink the fly.

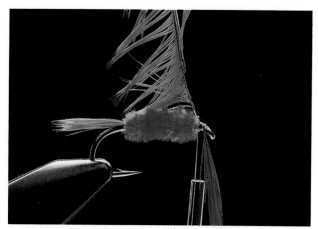

2 Fold hackle feather; then tie in tip just in front of body material. Make several turns of thread to secure. Trim off excess hackle tip.

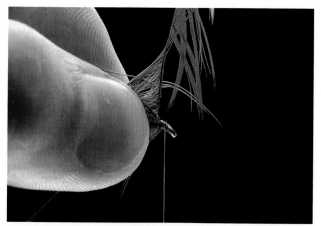

3 Wrap hackle once around shank of hook, then stroke fibers back with fingers.

4 Make two more wraps, stroking fibers back after each wrap. Make several turns of thread to secure. Trim excess hackle stem.

Palmered Hackle

Palmered hackle is wrapped in an open spiral over body materials, such as floss, chenille or dubbing. It should be the same length as dry-fly hackle, or slightly shorter.

Some flytiers wrap fine copper-wire ribbing over palmered hackle for added strength and durability.

Grizzly hackle is palmered over peacock herl on this Griffith's Gnat

How to Tie In Palmered Hackle

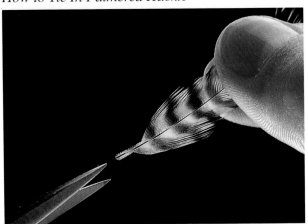

1 Select a dry-fly hackle feather of the proper size. Trim webbed portion.

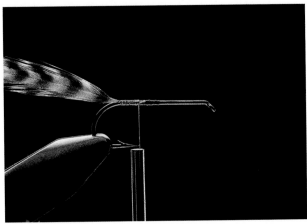

2 Place butt of hackle alongside hook shank at bend, with tip facing back. Secure with several turns of thread. Trim excess butt.

3 Tie in body material, wrap forward and secure.

4 Wind hackle forward over body in evenly spaced open spirals, using hackle pliers.

5 Secure hackle tip with thread; trim excess tip.

Parachute Hackle

Parachute hackle is wrapped horizontally around an upright wing of natural or synthetic fibers.

Although parachute hackle is the same length as dry-fly hackle, it is tied with only one hackle feather, instead of two.

Parachute hackle is wound horizontally around the base of the wing on this Light Cahill

How to Tie In Parachute Hackle

1 Tie in an upright, parachute-style wing (p. 65). Select a dry-fly hackle feather of proper size, and trim webbed portion.

2 Position hackle feather alongside hook shank at base of wing. Tie in hackle feather, shiny side up, with tip pointing back.

3 Grasp tip with hackle pliers and wrap hackle three times around base of wing to form horizontal collar.

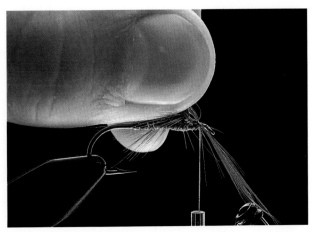

4 Pull hackle fibers back gently with fingers, so you can tie off without wrapping over hackle. Make several thread turns around stem and shank to secure. Trim excess hackle tip.

Finishing Knots

Before you trim off the thread and remove the fly from the vise, you must secure the thread using either a half-hitch or a whip-finish knot. The half-hitch is easier to learn but the whip-finish knot will last longer. Most flytiers use a special tool for the whip-finish knot, but you can easily tie a half-hitch without any special tools, as shown below (bare hook used for demonstration purposes).

How to Tie a Half-hitch Finishing Knot

1 Hold bobbin in left hand with 6 to 8 inches of thread between bobbin and hook eye. Spread first and second fingers of right hand, and place them against thread with palm facing away from you.

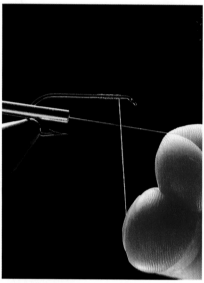

2 Twist right hand as you raise bobbin, forming a loop. Keep thread against fingertips, so palm is facing toward you and bobbin is horizontal.

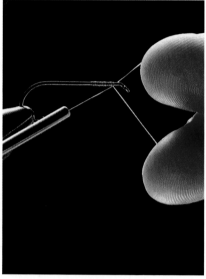

3 Begin to raise loop, hooking the thread beneath hook eye. Remove second finger from loop.

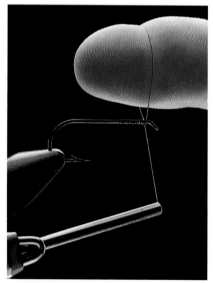

4 Raise loop over head of fly. Carefully remove first finger.

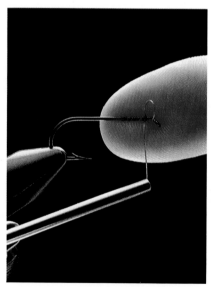

5 Slowly close loop by pulling down on bobbin. Repeat steps 1 through 5 several times. Trim excess thread.

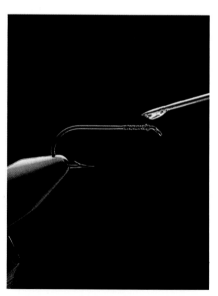

6 Apply a small amount of head cement to completed half-hitches for added strength.

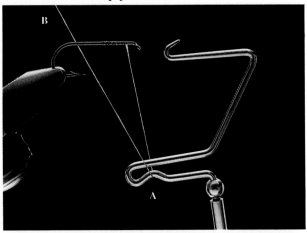

1 Hold bobbin in left hand with 6 to 8 inches of thread between bobbin and hook eye. Place bend of tool (A) against thread. Raise bobbin to position (B).

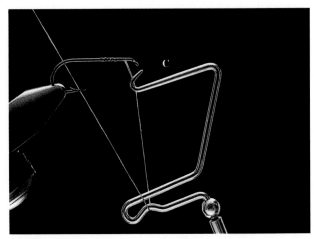

2 Catch thread with hook of tool (C) as shown.

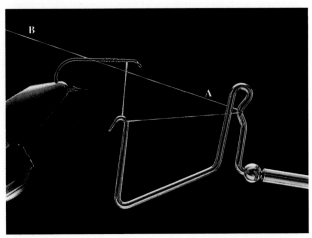

3 Lift handle to the right and rotate tool 180 degrees, keeping tension on thread. The thread (A to B) should be nearly parallel to shank.

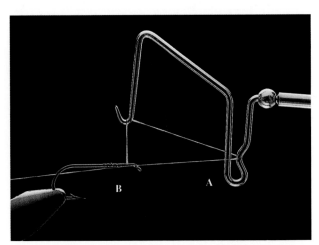

4 Rotate tool around shank five times, trapping thread (A to B) against shank.

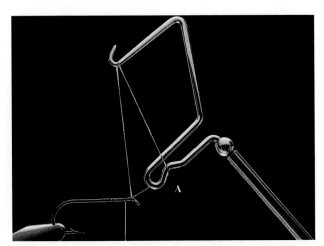

5 Raise tool above shank to free thread from bend (A). Do not release tension on thread.

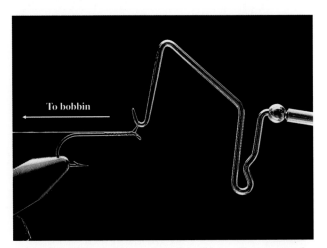

6 Pull bobbin slowly to close thread loop. Remove tool from thread and tug on bobbin to tighten knot. Trim excess thread and apply head cement to knot. The tag end is now covered with wraps, making the knot very secure.

Fly Patterns

Once you have learned to tie the basic parts of a fly — tail, body, wings and hackle — you can combine them to create a complete pattern. But first you should know how to read a fly-pattern recipe.

Any chef will tell you that the first ingredient listed in a recipe is the first to go into the dish. A fly-pattern recipe is no different.

The fly recipes in this book (sample below) begin with (1) hook, including style and size. The style portion lists a recommended hook, including manufacturer and model number, although you can substitute many other similar hooks. The size designation after the semicolon lists the size range in which the pattern is most commonly tied. The (2) thread listing gives you the recommended thread color and size. The recipe also lists the fly parts, such as (3) wing, (4) tail, (5) body and (6) hackle, in the order in which they are tied in.

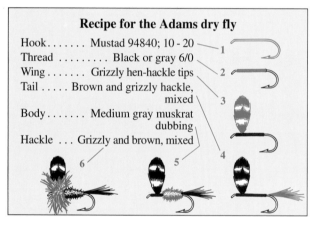

Recipe for the Adams dry fly

Hook......	Mustad 94840; 10 - 20
Thread	Black or gray 6/0
Wing	Grizzly hen-hackle tips
Tail	Brown and grizzly hackle, mixed
Body.......	Medium gray muskrat dubbing
Hackle ...	Grizzly and brown, mixed

In this section, you will learn to tie the six basic fly patterns, including a streamer, a nymph, a dry fly, a wet fly, a terrestrial and a bass fly. Following the instructions for each basic pattern are several pages showing recipes for many other flies of the same type.

Keep in mind that many popular fly patterns are tied in different fly types. In the fly catalogs that follow, for instance, you'll find recipes for a March Brown in dry-fly, wet-fly and nymph versions. You'll even find variations in materials and elements used in a specific pattern, depending on the region and the flytier. A Light Cahill wet fly, for example, can be tied with a tail of duck flank or hackle fibers; the Light Cahill dry, an upright-and-divided hackle-fiber wing, or a parachute-style hair wing.

Streamers

A streamer is designed to imitate a baitfish rather than an insect. Traditional streamers have hackle-feather wings that extend back, or "stream," over the body of the fly.

Another popular type of streamer is the *bucktail*, which has hair wings, making it more durable.

Both types can be extremely productive for salmon, trout, steelhead, bass and even pike.

Some streamer patterns, called imitators, closely resemble a real baitfish. Others, called attractors, use flash, color and movement to draw a strike.

Streamers are generally tied on extra-long hooks to help give them the long profile of a baitfish.

Streamers and bucktails are often weighted with lead wire, and are fished deep by casting them with a weighted line, or trolling.

Streamers can be retrieved upstream or down, or across the current with a jerky, twitching retrieve to simulate a baitfish.

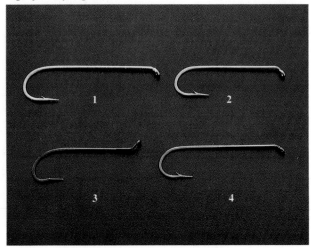

POPULAR HOOKS include: (1) TMC 5263; (2) Mustad 9672, (3) 9049X and (4) 79580.

BUILD a mound of thread, if needed, just behind the eye. The eye of some streamer hooks is slightly open; without a mound, materials could slip into, or snag on, the eye.

Fly-tying courses often begin with a streamer or bucktail pattern. Their large size and simple construction make these patterns easy to tie.

Many fly anglers believe that eyes increase the effectiveness of a streamer. Dab on eyes with a small dowel dipped in white acrylic paint. Use a smaller dowel to dab on the black pupil.

One classic, but still popular and effective, bucktail pattern is the Mickey Finn (below). Designed by John Alden Knight in the 1930s, it was named for the infamous drugged drink.

The Mickey Finn is an excellent baitfish imitation. The red stripe of bucktail resembles the lateral line of a small minnow or trout. Instructions for tying the Mickey Finn are on the following pages.

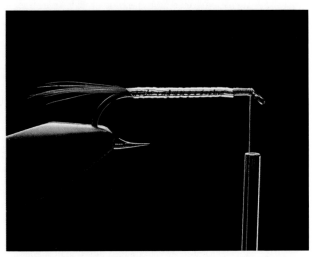

PAINT ON eyes, then dip the head into clear gloss lacquer. After lacquer dries, clean hook eye with dubbing needle.

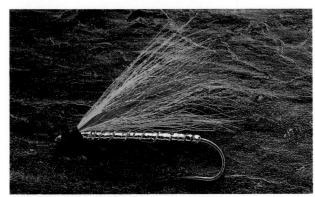

The Mickey Finn bucktail

How to Tie a Streamer: the Mickey Finn

Recipe

Hook . . . . Mustad 9672; 2 - 12
Thread . . . . Black 3/0
Weight (optional) . . Fine lead wire
Ribbing . . . . Oval silver tinsel
Body . . . . Flat silver tinsel
Wing . . . . Yellow and red bucktail, or calf tail

How to Tie the Mickey Finn

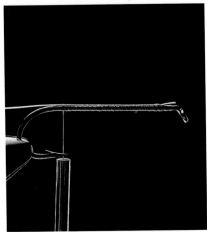

1 Tie in a 4-inch length of oval silver tinsel ribbing on top of hook shank, starting thread just behind hook eye and wrapping back to bend to secure tinsel.

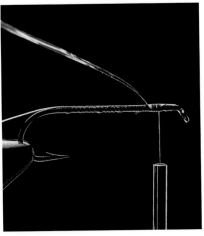

2 Wind thread forward again to tie-in point behind hook eye. Tie in a 6-inch length of flat silver tinsel body material.

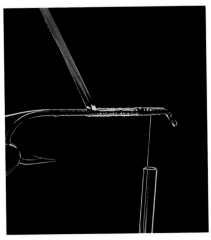

3 Wrap flat tinsel back to bend of hook. Each wrap should touch prevous wrap so there are no gaps.

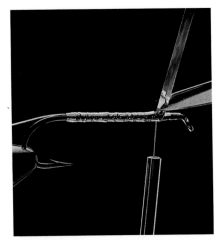

4 Reverse direction and wrap tinsel forward to tie-in point, overlapping first layer. Secure with several turns of thread.

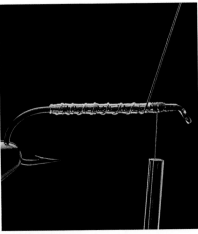

5 Wrap ribbing on hook, starting near bend, and wrap forward.

6 Cut a small bundle of yellow bucktail, and another of red. Comb out underfur with dubbing needle.

7 Stack bucktail fibers to align tips. Divide yellow bucktail into two equal bundles.

8 Measure first bundle to approximately 1½ times
hook-shank length.

9 Tie in first bundle of yellow bucktail with several soft
loops. Apply moderate thread tension for first few
wraps, then increase tension for several more wraps. If you
are having problems getting bucktail to stay on top of hook,
reduce amount of bucktail.

10 Trim butt ends of bucktail at an upward angle,
as shown; then wrap thread forward to cover tapered ends.

11 Measure bundle of red bucktail to same length as
first yellow bundle and place it directly on top of
yellow bundle. Tie in as in steps 9 and 10.

12 Measure second bundle of yellow to same length
as first and tie in as in steps 9 and 10. Whip-finish,
and apply head cement.

Catalog of Streamers

Black-nosed Dace

Hook.................. Mustad 9672; 4-12
Thread .... Black 6/0
Tail .... Red yarn
Rib .... Oval silver tinsel
Body......................... Flat silver tinsel
Wing............... Brown over black over
white bucktail

Royal Coachman Bucktail

Hook .... Mustad 3666; 10-16
Thread .... Black 6/0
Tail............... Golden pheasant tippet
Rib .... Fine gold wire
Butt .... Peacock herl
Body .... Red floss
Thorax .... Peacock herl
Hackle .... Dark brown hen
Wing .... White bucktail

Llama

Hook.................. Mustad 9673; 4-10
Thread........................... Black 6/0
Rib .... Flat gold tinsel or Mylar
Body..................... Red wool yarn
Wing..................... Woodchuck hair
Hackle........................ Grizzly hen

Light Spruce

Hook.................. Mustad 9672; 2-10
Thread .... Black 6/0
Tail .... Peacock sword fibers
Rib .... Fine copper wire
Body.............. Rear half red wool yarn,
front half peacock herl
Wing...... Two badger-colored saddle hackles
Hackle .... Badger saddle

Silver Darter

Hook .... Mustad 9672; 4-10
Thread .... Black 6/0
Tag......... Red monocord, to secure end of
body tubing
Body.............. Silver Mylar body tubing
Beard .... Peacock sword fibers
Wing .... Badger saddle

Pass Lake

Hook.................. Mustad 9672; 8-12
Thread........................... Black 6/0
Tail .... Brown hen hackle fibers
Body..................... Black chenille
Hackle........................ Brown hen
Wing..................... White calf tail

Grizzly King

Hook.................. Mustad 9672; 4-12
Thread .... Black 6/0
Tail .... Red hackle fibers
Rib .... Fine flat silver tinsel
Body......................... Green floss
Beard .... Grizzly or dun hackle fibers
Wing........................ Grizzly saddle

Black Matuka

Hook .... Mustad 9672; 2-10
Thread .... Black 6/0
Rib .... Fine copper wire
Body .... Black chenille
Wing ..... Four black hen saddle hackles, tied
down over body with rib
Hackle .... Black hen

Byford's White Zonker

Hook..................... Mustad 9672; 2-6
Thread........................... White 6/0
Weight........................ Lead wire
Body .... Pearl Mylar body tubing
Wing and Tail .... White rabbit strip,
glued to body
Topping................. Pearl Krystal Flash
Beard .... White rabbit dubbing
Eyes .... Painted yellow with black pupil

Gray Ghost

Hook . . . . Mustad 79580; 2-10
Thread . . . . Black 6/0
Tag and Rib . . . . Strand of fine flat silver tinsel
Body . . . . Orange floss
Beard . . . . . Four strands of peacock herl, white, bucktail, golden pheasant crest
Underwing . . . . Golden pheasant crest
Wing . . . . Four gray dun saddle hackles
Sides . . . . . . Two silver pheasant body feathers
Cheeks . . . . Jungle cock (optional)

Black Ghost

Hook . . . . Mustad 79580; 2-6
Thread . . . . Black 6/0
Tail . . . . Yellow hackle fibers
Rib . . . . Medium flat silver tinsel
Body . . . . Black floss
Beard . . . . Yellow hackle fibers
Wing . . . . Four white saddle hackles
Cheeks . . . . Jungle cock (optional)

Supervisor

Hook . . . . Mustad 79580; 2-10
Thread . . . . Black 6/0
Tail . . . . Red wool yarn, short
Rib . . . . Medium oval silver tinsel
Body . . . . Flat silver tinsel
Beard . . . . White hackle fibers
Wing . . . . White bucktail with four blue saddle hackles
Sides . . . . Two green saddle hackles
Topping . . . . Peacock herl
Cheeks . . . . Jungle cock (optional)

Purple Woolly Bugger

Hook . . . . Mustad 9672; 2-12
Thread . . . . Black 6/0
Tail . . . . Purple marabou
Rib . . . . Fine copper wire (optional)
Body . . . . Purple chenille
Hackle . . . . Black, palmered over body

Lead-eyed Egg Leech

Hook . . . . Mustad 9672; 4-8
Thread . . . . Black 6/0
Tail . . . . Black rabbit fur strip
Body . . . . Black rabbit fur strip, wrapped
Eyes . . . . Nickel-plated hourglass eyes
Thorax . . . . Black rabbit dubbing
Head . . . . Fluorescent hot pink chenille

Muddler Minnow

Hook . . . . Mustad 9672; 2-14
Thread . . . . Black 6/0
Tail . . . . Mottled turkey wing quill segment
Body . . . . Gold tinsel
Underwing . . . . Gray squirrel tail
Wing . . . . Mottled turkey quill
Collar . . . . Natural deer hair, spun
Head . . . . . . Natural deer hair, spun and clipped

Black Marabou Muddler

Hook . . . . Mustad 9672; 2-10
Thread . . . . Black 6/0
Tail . . . . Red hackle fibers
Body . . . . Silver tinsel
Wing . . . . . . Black marabou with six strands of peacock herl
Collar . . . . Deer hair, spun
Head . . . . Deer hair, spun and clipped

Olive Whit's Sculpin

Hook . . . . Mustad 9672; 1/0-8
Thread . . . . Olive 3/0
Rib . . . . Medium oval gold tinsel
Body . . . . Light olive wool yarn
Thorax . . . . Red wool dubbing
Wing . . . . Two olive grizzly hackles, tied to body with ribbing
Fins . . . . Olive hen mallard breast
Collar . . . . . . Olive deer hair, spun and clipped
Head . . . . Olive deer hair with a band of black deer hair, spun and clipped

Wool Shad

Hook . . . . TMC 5263; 2-10
Thread . . . . Gray 3/0
Wing . . . . Silver Krystal Flash over white marabou
Sides . . . . Grizzly saddle hackles, splayed
Body . . . . Gray thread
Collar . . . . Grizzly saddle hackle
Head . . . . Wool dubbing, clipped to shape
Eyes . . . Hourglass eyes, white with black pupils

Nymphs

Designed to be fished below the surface, a nymph is usually tied on a hook that is slightly heavier than a dry-fly hook, and is often productive even when fish do not appear to be feeding.

Nymphs make up the second largest fly-pattern category, next to dry flies, and are an important part of any flytier's repertoire.

Anglers use the term "nymph" when referring to any of the larval, pupal and nymphal stages of aquatic insects. In fly tying, the term refers to imitations of these forms, or to imitations of crustaceans, such as scuds, shrimp and sometimes crayfish.

Nymphs are effective not only for trout, but also for panfish and bass. With immature aquatic insects and crustaceans making up a significant portion of the diet of most gamefish, as much as 90 percent in the case of trout, it's not surprising that nymphs work so well.

Not all nymph patterns are exact imitations. Some, called searching patterns, are impressionistic, suggesting a number of food items rather than a specific

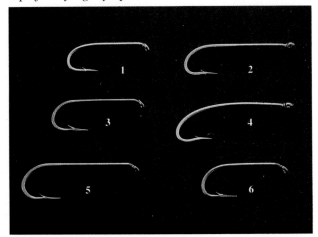

POPULAR HOOKS include: (1) TMC 3761, (2) TMC 939S, (3) Mustad 9671, (4) TMC 200R, (5) Mustad 9672 and (6) Mustad 3906.

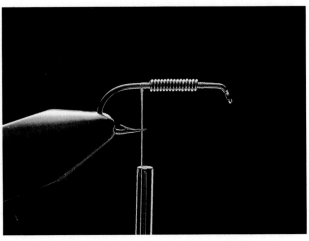

ADD weight to center of hook shank to make fly sink horizontally.

APPLY a few drops of head cement to wingcase feather to keep fibers together on completed wingcase.

DUB thorax thicker than abdomen to create a realistic profile and provide enough material for plucking out legs.

one. These patterns are a good choice when it is difficult to determine exactly which naturals the fish are eating.

Nymph patterns range in size from tiny imitations of midge larvae to large stonefly patterns. They can be tied using natural and synthetic materials in a variety of colors, shapes and sizes, depending on the naturals.

Nymphs should be fished at the depth that fish are taking the naturals. When fish are feeding deep, use a weighted nymph or add a split shot to your leader a few feet from the fly. Use an unweighted nymph for fishing just below the surface.

One of the most popular and effective nymphs is the Gold-ribbed Hare's Ear (right and following pages). Its general profile and color are similar to many different species of mayfly, making it an excellent

searching pattern all season long. Weight the pattern, if desired, by adding a brass bead (p. 42).

The Hare's Ear gets its unusual name from the soft, absorbent fibers of a hare's mask (p. 25), used for the body and tail of the fly.

The Gold-ribbed Hare's Ear nymph

How to Tie a Nymph: The Gold-ribbed Hare's Ear

Recipe	
Hook	Mustad 3906; 8 - 16
Thread	Tan or brown 6/0
Tail. . . .	Hare's mask guard hairs, or brown hackle fibers
Rib	Fine oval gold tinsel, or copper wire
Body	Hare's mask dubbing, thorax thicker than abdomen
Wingcase	Mottled turkey, or goose wing-quill segment

How to Tie a Gold-ribbed Hare's Ear Nymph

1 Start thread at midpoint of hook shank and wind back to bend. Tie in 10 to 15 hare's mask fibers at bend to form tail. Wind thread forward to middle of shank and trim any excess butts.

2 Tie in a two-inch length of fine oval gold tinsel ribbing and wrap thread over tinsel to hook bend. Trim off any tinsel that extends forward.

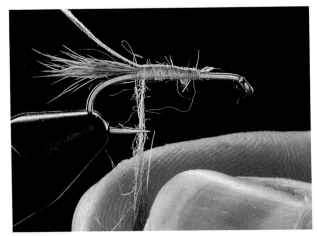

3 Apply hare's mask dubbing to thread.

4 Wind the dubbed thread forward to middle of shank to form tapered body.

5 Wrap tinsel forward to middle of shank with four or five open-spiral turns. Secure with several turns of thread, and trim off tag end of tinsel.

6 Snip a ½-inch-wide quill segment from a large mottled turkey or goose wing feather for wingcase.

7 Tie in quill segment, shiny side up, with tip toward bend. Make several turns of thread to secure.

8 Snip off butt end of segment, then wind thread forward over trimmed end to secure. Wind thread back to wing tie-in point.

9 Apply a generous amount of hare's mask dubbing to thread, then wind dubbed thread forward to about one hook-eye length behind eye to form thorax.

10 Pull end of quill segment over thorax to form wing-case. Secure wingcase with several turns of thread, and trim excess. Form head, whip-finish and apply head cement to knot and wingcase. Pluck out fibers from thorax, if desired, to form legs.

Catalog of Nymphs

Pheasant Tail Nymph

Hook	Mustad 9671; 10-18
Thread	Brown 6/0
Tail	Pheasant tail fibers
Rib	Fine copper wire
Body	Pheasant tail fibers, wrapped herl-style
Wingcase	Pheasant tail fibers
Thorax	Peacock herl

Breadcrust Nymph

Hook	Mustad 3906; 8-14
Thread	Black 6/0
Rib	Stripped ruffed grouse tail feather, and fine copper wire
Body	Burnt orange rabbit dubbing
Hackle	Grizzly hen

Dark Hendrickson Nymph

Hook	Mustad 3906B; 10-14
Thread	Olive 6/0
Tail	Lemon wood duck fibers
Rib	Brown floss
Abdomen	Red fox dubbing
Wingcase	White-tip turkey tail segment
Thorax	Red fox dubbing
Sides	Brown partridge

Blue-wing Olive Nymph

Hook	Mustad 9671; 14-18
Thread	Olive 6/0
Tail	Lemon wood duck flank fibers
Rib	Brown silk thread
Body	Medium olive rabbit dubbing
Wingcase	Goose wing quill fibers
Thorax	Medium olive rabbit dubbing
Legs	Brown partridge hackle fibers

Isonychia Nymph

Hook	Mustad 9671; 10-16
Thread	Red 6/0
Tail	Pheasant tail fibers
Shellback	Stripped white hackle stem over top of body and wingcase, tied in with rib
Rib	Black floss
Body	Dark red-brown dubbing
Wingcase	Dark quill segment
Thorax	Dark red-brown dubbing
Sides	Wood duck flank fibers

Quill Gordon Nymph

Hook	Mustad 9671; 10-14
Thread	Olive 6/0
Tail	Two pheasant tail fibers
Rib	Brown thread
Body	Beaver dubbing
Wingcase	Mottled turkey wing quill
Thorax	Beaver dubbing
Beard	Brown partridge fibers

Black Quill Nymph

Hook	Mustad 9671; 10-14
Thread	Black 6/0
Tail	Medium dun hackle fibers
Body	Stripped peacock herl
Wingcase	Dark mallard wing-quill segment
Thorax	Muskrat dubbing
Beard	Medium blue dun hen

Red Squirrel Nymph

Hook	Mustad 9672; 6-10
Thread	Black 6/0
Tail	Hare's mask guard hair
Body	Red squirrel dubbing
Rib	Fine oval gold tinsel
Thorax	Dark gray Antron dubbing

March Brown Nymph

Hook	Mustad 9671; 12-18
Thread	Rust 6/0
Tail	Pheasant tail fibers
Rib	Brown thread
Body	Red fox and amber goat dubbing
Wingcase	Mottled turkey quill segment
Thorax	Red fox and amber goat dubbing
Sides	Partridge hackle

Flashabou Nymph

Hook . . . . Mustad 3906B; 10-18
Thread . . . . Black 6/0
Tail. . . . . Ringneck pheasant tail fibers
Body . . . . Pearl Flashabou, wrapped
Wingcase . . . . Pearl Flashabou
Thorax . . . . Black rabbit and goat dubbing

Prince Nymph

Hook . . . . Mustad 9671; 4-10
Thread . . . . Black 6/0
Tail . . . . Brown goose biots
Rib . . . . Fine flat gold tinsel
Body . . . . Peacock herl
Hackle . . . . Brown
Wing . . . . White biots tied in with tips
facing back

Tellico Nymph

Hook . . . . Mustad 9671; 12-16
Thread . . . . Black 6/0
Tail. . . . . Guinea body fibers
Shellback . . . . Ringneck pheasant tail fibers
Rib . . . . Peacock herl
Body . . . . Yellow floss
Hackle . . . . Furnace-colored hackle

Zug Bug

Hook . . . . TMC 3761; 8-16
Thread . . . . Black 6/0
Tail. . . . . Peacock sword fibers
Body . . . . Peacock herl
Hackle . . . . Brown, wet-fly style
Wingcase . . . . Lemon wood duck flank

Montana Stone

Hook . . . . Mustad 9672; 6-10
Thread . . . . Black 6/0
Tail . . . . Brown goose biots
Body . . . . Brown chenille
Wingcase . . . . Brown chenille
Thorax . . . . Orange chenille
Hackle . . . . Black, palmered over thorax

Bitch Creek

Hook . . . . Mustad 9672; 2-10
Thread . . . . Black 6/0
Tail. . . . . White rubber strips
Body . . . . Black and orange chenille
Rib . . . . Fine gold wire, over thorax
Thorax . . . . Black chenille
Hackle . . . . Brown, palmered over thorax
Antennae . . . . White rubber strips

Damselfly Nymph

Hook . . . . Mustad 9671; 8-12
Thread . . . . Olive 6/0
Tail. . . . . Olive marabou
Body . . . . Green yarn or dubbing
Rib . . . . Oval gold tinsel
Eyes . . . . Black hourglass
Thorax and Head . . . . . . Green yarn or dubbing
Sides . . . . Green grizzly hen
Wingcase . . . . Olive Swiss Straw, folded

Green Drake Nymph

Hook . . . . Mustad 9672; 10-12
Thread . . . . Olive 6/0
Tail . . . . Mahogany ringneck pheasant tail fibers
Rib . . . . Olive floss
Abdomen . . . . Olive-tan dubbing
Wingcase . . . . . . White-tip turkey tail segment
Thorax . . . . Olive-tan dubbing
Sides . . . . Lemon wood duck fibers

Hexagenia Nymph

Hook . . . . Mustad 9672; 4-10
Thread . . . . Olive 6/0
Tail. . . . . Barred olive marabou
Rib . . . . Fine copper wire
Body . . . . Medium brown dubbing
Wingcase . . . . Mottled turkey
Thorax . . . . Medium brown dubbing
Legs . . . . Barred olive marabou
Eyes . . . . Monofilament
Antennae . . . . Barred olive marabou

Hellgrammite

Hook (upside down)................... Mustad 79580; 2-8
Thread .... Brown 6/0
Tail .... Brown goose biots
Shellback .... Ringneck pheasant tail fibers
Rib .... Fine copper wire
Body............... Brown Antron dubbing, picked out on the sides
Wingcase .... Ringneck pheasant tail fibers
Thorax .... Brown Antron dubbing, picked out on the sides
Legs .... Speckled hen saddle, pulled over thorax
Antennae .... Brown goose biots

Giant Black Stonefly Nymph

Hook .... TMC 200R; 2-8
Thread .... Black 6/0
Tail .... Black goose biots
Rib .... Black Larva Lace
Body............... Black rabbit dubbing or synthetic hair
Wingcase .... Three turkey-quill segments tied in over thorax
Thorax .... Black rabbit dubbing
Legs .... Thorax dubbing, plucked out with dubbing needle
Head......................... Black rabbit dubbing
Antennae .... Black goose biots

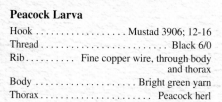

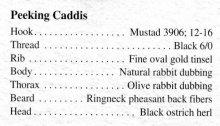

Brassie

Hook.................. Mustad 9671; 10-18
Thread .... Black 6/0
Body.......................... Copper wire
Thorax .... Gray muskrat dubbing, with guard hairs

Peacock Larva

Hook .... Mustad 3906; 12-16
Thread .... Black 6/0
Rib .... Fine copper wire, through body and thorax
Body .... Bright green yarn
Thorax .... Peacock herl
Beard .... Two short strands of peacock herl

Peeking Caddis

Hook.................. Mustad 3906; 12-16
Thread .... Black 6/0
Rib .... Fine oval gold tinsel
Body.............. Natural rabbit dubbing
Thorax .... Olive rabbit dubbing
Beard .... Ringneck pheasant back fibers
Head................... Black ostrich herl

Olive Larva

Hook.................. TMC 200R; 12-16
Thread .... Brown 6/0
Rib .... Fine gold wire
Body........................ Olive dubbing
Beard .... Brown partridge hackle
Head.......... Dark brown rabbit dubbing

Speckled Sedge

Hook .... Mustad 3906; 12-16
Thread .... Brown 6/0
Rib ...... Reddish brown Australian opossum, tightly dubbed onto thread to make ribbing
Body .... Light brown mink dubbing
Wing .... Gray duck wing-quill segments
Beard .... Brown partridge hackle
Head .... Dark brown rabbit dubbing

Olive Sedge

Hook .... Mustad 3906; 14-18
Thread......................... Brown 6/0
Body..................... Pale olive dubbing
Wingcase ... Natural gray duck-quill segments
Beard .... Brown partridge hackle
Head .... Dark brown rabbit dubbing

GLF Cased Caddis

Hook	TMC 100; 8-14
Thread	Brown 6/0
Body	Dark brown and gray grouse hackles wrapped herl-style, clipped
Thorax	Pale olive rabbit dubbing
Beard	Dark brown and gray hackle fibers
Head	Black dubbing (optional)

GLF Emerging Caddis

Hook	TMC 100; 12-18
Thread	Black 6/0
Tail	Antron fibers from body
Underbody	Gold Antron dubbing and brown rabbit dubbing
Body	Tan Antron yarn
Wing	Dark speckled deer hair
Head	Brown rabbit dubbing

Deep Sparkling Pupa

Hook	TMC 100; 12-18
Thread	Black 6/0
Underbody	One-half olive, one-half bright green Antron
Body	Medium olive Antron yarn
Hackle	Grouse

Goplin Emerger

Hook	TMC 100; 12-20
Thread	Brown 6/0
Tail	Brown hackle fibers
Body	Tan dubbing
Wingcase	Gray hen-hackle fibers, tied to form loop
Legs	Gray hen-hackle fibers cut from loop, each side
Thorax	Tan dubbing

Floating Nymph

Hook	TMC 100; 12-20
Thread	Olive 6/0
Tail	Dun hackle fibers
Rib	Tan thread
Body	Olive dubbing
Wingcase	Brown dubbing spun onto thread, then pushed down onto top of thorax to form ball
Beard	Dun hackle fibers

CDC Hendrickson Emerger

Hook	TMC 100; 12-20
Thread	Brown 6/0
Tail	Lemon wood duck flank fibers
Rib	Fine copper wire
Body	Brown Antron dubbing
Wing	Dun CDC feathers, tied in at sides
Legs	Partridge hackle
Head	Brown Antron

Olive Scud

Hook	TMC 200R; 10-18
Thread	Brown 6/0
Tail	Olive hackle fibers
Rib	Black thread
Body	Mixed olive rabbit and goat dubbing, picked out on bottom
Shellback	Clear plastic
Antennae	Olive hackle fibers

Big Horn Scud

Hook	Mustad 3906; 8-16
Thread	Orange 6/0
Tail	Ringneck pheasant tail fibers
Rib	Copper wire
Body	Yellow Antron dubbing, picked out on underside
Shellback	Clear plastic

Sow Bug

Hook	Mustad 3906; 10-16
Thread	Gray 6/0
Tail	Gray goose biots
Rib	Fine silver wire
Body	Muskrat dubbing
Legs	Fibers, picked out from body dubbing

Bead-head Prince

Hook . . . . TMC 3761; 8-16
Thread . . . . Red 6/0
Head . . . . Brass bead
Tail . . . . Brown goose biots
Rib . . . . Gold Mylar
Body . . . . Peacock herl
Wing . . . . White goose biots
Hackle . . . . Brown hen

2¹/₂-week Caddis

Hook . . . . TMC 206BL; 14-18
Thread . . . . Olive 6/0
Head . . . . Brass bead
Body . . . . Micro chenille, with singed end
Wing . . . . Tan CDC
Sides . . . . Mallard wing-quill segments
Thorax . . . . Peacock herl

Bead-head Hare's Ear

Hook . . . . TMC 3761; 10-18
Thread . . . . Black 6/0
Head . . . . Copper bead
Tail . . . . Hare's mask guard hair
Rib . . . . Gold flat Mylar
Body . . . . Hare's mask dubbing
Legs . . . . Hare's mask guard hair

Bead-head Caddis Pupa

Hook . . . . TMC 3761; 10-18
Thread . . . . Olive 6/0
Head . . . . Brass bead
Body . . . . Olive rabbit dubbing
Hackle . . . . Brown partridge
Wing . . . . Ringneck pheasant tail fibers

Bead-head Pheasant Tail

Hook . . . . TMC 2457; 10-18
Thread . . . . Brown 6/0
Head . . . . Brass bead
Tail . . . . Pheasant tail fibers
Rib . . . . Copper wire
Body . . . . Ringneck pheasant tail fibers,
wrapped herl-style

Pete's Pheasant Caddis

Hook . . . . TMC 2457; 10-18
Thread . . . . Black 6/0
Head . . . . Brass bead
Rib . . . . Fine gold wire
Thorax . . . . Peacock herl
Body . . . . Pheasant tail fibers
Beard . . . . Pheasant tail or partridge

Bead-head Rabbit Emerger

Hook . . . . TMC 2457; 12-16
Thread . . . . Red 6/0
Head . . . . Brass bead
Tail . . . . White Z-lon or Antron yarn
Body . . . . Dark brown rabbit dubbing
Wing . . . . White calf tail
Thorax . . . . Dark brown rabbit dubbing

Brassie

Hook . . . . TMC 2457; 14-18
Thread . . . . Black 6/0
Head . . . . Copper bead
Body . . . . Copper wire
Thorax . . . . Peacock herl

Bead-head Serendipity

Hook . . . . TMC 2457; 12-18
Thread . . . . Red 6/0
Head . . . . Brass bead
Body . . . . . Red Z-lon or Antron yarn, twisted
to form a thin strand
Wing . . . . White deer hair, trimmed short

Bead-butt Scud

Hook	TMC 2457; 8-16
Thread	Orange 6/0
Tail	Pheasant-tail fibers
Rib	Amber V-rib
Body	Orange Antron dubbing
Shellback	Clear plastic or pearl Mylar
Butt	Brass bead, slid over tail at hook bend

Bottle Brush

Hook	TMC 2457; 10-16
Thread	Tan 6/0
Head	Copper bead
Tail	Two goose biots
Body	Natural rabbit hair, twisted with copper wire or thread
Beard	Partridge hackle

Van's Case Caddis

Hook	TMC 2487; 12-18
Thread	Olive 6/0
Head	Copper bead
Underbody	Olive hare's mask dubbing
Body	Black and yellow Swiss Straw, clipped randomly
Beard	Partridge hackle
Thorax	Olive hare's mask dubbing

Theo's Danger Baby

Hook	TMC 2457; 8-16
Thread	Black 6/0
Head	Brass bead
Tag	Fluorescent chartreuse thread
Rib	Fine gold wire
Body	Peacock herl
Wing	Light olive Z-lon, caddis-style
Thorax	Peacock herl

Peacock Bead-head

Hook	TMC 2457; 12-18
Thread	Black 6/0
Head	Brass bead
Tag	Fluorescent chartreuse thread
Rib	Fine gold wire
Body	Peacock herl

Gold-bead Possie Nymph

Hook	TMC 2457; 8-14
Thread	Gray 6/0
Head	Brass bead
Tail	Australian opossum guard hairs
Rib	Fine copper wire
Body	Australian opossum dubbing
Thorax	Australian opossum guard hairs

Thunderhead

Hook	Mustad 9672; 6-12
Thread	Black 6/0
Head	Nickel bead
Beard	Chartreuse synthetic hair or bucktail, tied length of wing
Wing	Synthetic hair or bucktail, purple over black
Rib	Oval gold tinsel
Body	Flat silver Mylar

Bead-head Stonefly

Hook	Mustad 9672; 4-10
Thread	Brown 6/0
Head	Brass bead
Thorax	Brown rabbit dubbing
Hackle	Brown
Weight	Brass bead, tied in behind thorax
Tail	Amber goose biots
Rib	Copper wire
Body	Brown rabbit dubbing
Wingcase	Mottled turkey, folded

Bead-head Giant Black Stonefly

Hook	TMC 200R; 2-10
Thread	Black 6/0
Head	Brass bead
Tail	Black goose biots
Rib	Black Larva Lace
Body	Black Antron dubbing
Wingcase	Black Swiss Straw, folded over thorax
Thorax	Black Antron dubbing
Legs	Dubbing, plucked from thorax

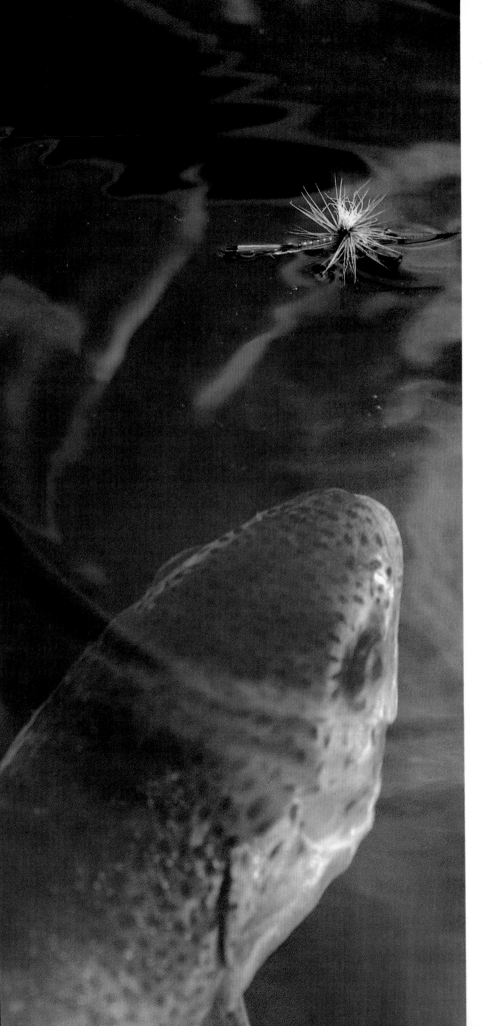

Dry Flies

Designed to float on the surface, a dry fly is usually tied on a light-wire hook, and balances on the fibers of its tail and hackle.

Dry flies make up the largest and most diverse category of fly patterns. It includes attractors tied in bright colors; impressionistic searching patterns; and imitators, which mimic the adult forms of various aquatic insects, such as mayflies, caddisflies, midges and stoneflies.

Dry flies are designed primarily for fishing trout, which can be frustratingly selective in their feeding habits. This explains why flytiers have developed hundreds of dry-fly patterns.

When tying a dry fly to match a natural, consider size first. A pattern that is much larger than the natural may spook the fish.

Color is also important. Try to match that of the natural as closely as possible. Some materials, such as dubbing, will change color when they get wet. It's a good idea to choose a body material a few shades lighter than the color of the natural.

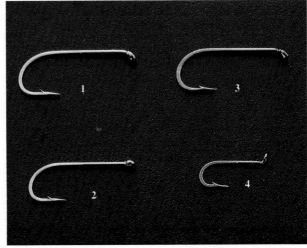

POPULAR HOOKS include: (1) TMC 100 and (2) 101; (3) Mustad 94840 and (4) 94842.

Other considerations are durability, buoyancy and visibility to the angler.

Flies made with hair wings and tails float well and stand up to rough water better than those with feather wings and tails.

Treating your flies with floatant helps them stay on the surface longer. Waterproofers (right) can be sprayed on newly tied flies for added flotation.

Flies that float high on the water are easier for the fisherman to see than those in the surface film. For low-riding flies, such as parachutes, use a light-colored or fluorescent wing material. In low-light situations, switch to a light-colored fly.

A favorite dry fly in many situations, the Adams (below and following pages) is a classic searching pattern. Designed in 1922 by Len Halladay for his friend C. F. Adams, it quickly became the most popular dry fly in America, and remains so today.

DRESS flies for slow or clear water (top) more sparsely than flies for rough or dirty water (bottom).

The Adams dry fly

TREAT finished flies with a waterproofer, such as Scotch-guard®, for long-lasting flotation.

How to Tie a Dry Fly: The Adams

Recipe	
Hook	Mustad 94840; 10 - 20
Thread	Gray or black, 6/0
Wing	Grizzly hen-hackle tips
Tail	Brown and grizzly hackle, mixed
Body	Medium gray muskrat dubbing
Hackle . . .	Brown and grizzly, mixed

How to Tie an Adams

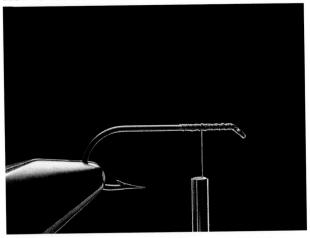

1 Start thread about one-third shank length behind eye and form a base for tying in wings.

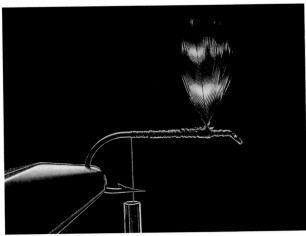

2 Tie in two hackle-point wings as shown on page 64. Wind thread back to hook bend.

3 Strip a small bunch of grizzly hackle fibers, and an equal bunch of brown hackle fibers, for the tail. Stack fibers so tips are aligned.

4 Tie in tail fibers at hook bend. Trim off excess butts and wind thread forward to secure. Wind thread back to bend.

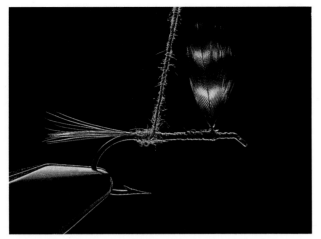

5 Apply a small amount of dubbing to thread. Wind dubbed thread forward.

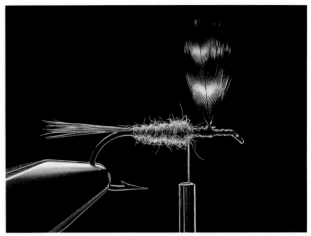

6 Form a tapered body, leaving a gap between body and wings for tying in and wrapping hackle.

7 Select one grizzly and one brown hackle feather of proper size, and trim webbing from base (p. 67).

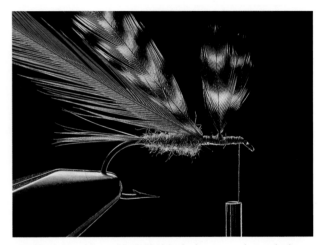

8 Tie in hackles with dull side facing you, tips pointing back. Make several turns of thread to secure hackles, and trim butt ends. Wrap thread forward to one hook-eye length behind eye.

9 Grasp tip of first hackle with hackle pliers. Wrap hackle forward, making three wraps behind wing, and three more in front. Secure hackle tip with thread. Repeat with second hackle.

10 Trim excess hackle feathers and any fibers that are trapped under thread turns. Form a head, whip-finish and apply head cement.

Catalog of Dry Flies

Adams
Hook................ Mustad 94840; 10-20
Thread....................... Black 6/0
Wing............... Grizzly hen-hackle tips
Tail .... Brown and grizzly hackle fibers, mixed
Body............... Gray muskrat dubbing
Hackle .... Brown and grizzly, mixed

Light Cahill
Hook .... TMC 100; 10-20
Thread .... Cream 6/0
Wing .... Lemon wood duck flank fibers
Tail.............. Light ginger hackle fibers
Body .... Cream dubbing
Hackle .... Light ginger

Light Hendrickson
Hook................ Mustad 94840; 12-18
Thread....................... Tan 6/0
Wing ...... Lemon wood duck flank fibers
Tail ...... Medium blue dun hackle fibers
Body .... Red fox dubbing
Hackle................. Medium blue dun

Dark Hendrickson
Hook............... Mustad 94840; 12-18
Thread .... Gray 6/0
Wing......... Lemon wood duck flank fibers
Tail .... Dark blue dun hackle fibers
Body .... Dark gray muskrat dubbing
Hackle .... Dark blue dun

Blue-wing Olive
Hook .... TMC 100; 12-20
Thread .... Olive 6/0
Wing .... Blue dun hen-hackle tips
Tail.................. Blue dun hackle fibers
Rib..................... Brown silk thread
Body .... Medium olive rabbit dubbing
Hackle .... Blue dun

Gray Fox Variant
Hook................ Mustad 94840; 12-14
Thread...................... Primrose 6/0
Wing .... Mallard flank fibers
Tail .... Golden ginger hackle fibers
Body .... Red fox dubbing
Hackle... Golden ginger and light grizzly, mixed,
oversized

Blue Dun
Hook................... TMC 100; 12-18
Thread .... Gray 6/0
Wing........ Natural gray duck quill segment
Tail .... Medium blue dun hackle fibers
Body .... Gray muskrat dubbing
Hackle .... Medium blue dun

March Brown
Hook .... Mustad 94840; 10-14
Thread .... Brown 6/0
Wing .... Turkey quill segment
Tail................. Dark ginger hackle fibers
Rib......... Yellow thread or gold oval tinsel
Body .... Brown rabbit dubbing
Hackle .... Dark ginger

Black Gnat
Hook.................. TMC 100; 12-20
Thread....................... Black 6/0
Wing .... Natural gray duck quill segment
Tail .... Black hackle fibers
Body .... Black rabbit dubbing
Hackle........................... Black

Mosquito

Hook . . . . TMC 100; 12-18
Thread . . . . Black 6/0
Wing . . . . Grizzly hen-hackle tips
Tail . . . . Grizzly hackle fibers
Body . . . . Moose mane, quill-style
Hackle . . . . Grizzly

Red Quill

Hook . . . . Mustad 94840; 12-16
Thread . . . . Gray 6/0
Wing . . . . Lemon wood duck flank fibers
Tail . . . . Medium bronze dun hackle fibers
Body . . . . Brown hackle stem, quill-style
Hackle . . . . Medium bronze dun

Quill Gordon

Hook . . . . Mustad 94840; 12-16
Thread . . . . Black 6/0
Wing . . . . Lemon wood duck flank fibers
Tail . . . . Dark blue dun hackle fibers
Body . . . . Stripped peacock herl
Hackle . . . . Dark blue dun

Royal Coachman

Hook . . . . Mustad 94840; 10-18
Thread . . . . Black 6/0
Wing . . . . White duck quill segments
Tail . . . . . . Golden pheasant tippet or coachman
brown hackle fibers
Body . . . . Peacock herl with red floss band
Hackle . . . . Coachman brown

Renegade

Hook . . . . TMC 100; 6-18
Thread . . . . Black 6/0
Tag . . . . Fine flat gold tinsel
Rear Hackle . . . . Brown
Body . . . . Peacock herl
Front Hackle . . . . White

Brown Bivisible

Hook . . . . Mustad 94840; 10-14
Thread . . . . Black 6/0
Tail . . . . Brown hackle fibers
Body . . . Brown hackle, wrapped in tight spirals
around rear two-thirds of shank
Hackle . . . . Cream

Blue Quill

Hook . . . . Mustad 94840; 12-18
Thread . . . . Black 6/0
Wing . . . . . . Natural gray duck quill segments
Tail . . . . Medium blue dun hackle fibers
Body . . . . Stripped peacock herl
Hackle . . . . Medium blue dun

Blue-wing Olive Parachute

Hook . . . . Mustad 94840; 12-20
Thread . . . . Olive 6/0
Wing . . . . Calf body hair, parachute-style
Tail . . . . Medium blue dun hackle fibers
Body . . . . Olive dubbing
Hackle . . . . Medium blue dun

Light Cahill Parachute

Hook . . . . TMC 100; 12-18
Thread . . . . Cream 6/0
Wing . . . . Calf body hair, parachute-style
Tail . . . . Light ginger hackle fibers
Body . . . . Cream dubbing
Hackle . . . . Light ginger

Pale Morning Dun

Hook . . . . TMC 100; 12-18
Thread . . . . Cream 6/0
Wing . . . . Light dun hen-hackle tips
Tail . . . . Light dun hackle fibers
Body . . . . Cream rabbit dubbing
Hackle . . . . Light dun

Pale Evening Dun

Hook . . . . Mustad 94840; 14-20
Thread . . . . Cream 6/0
Wing . . . . Light blue dun hen-hackle tips
Tail . . . . Light blue dun hackle fibers
Body . . . . Pale yellow rabbit dubbing
Hackle . . . . Medium blue dun

Sulphur Dun

Hook . . . . TMC 100; 16 -18
Thread . . . . Cream 6/0
Wing . . . . Cream hen-hackle tips
Tail . . . . Light blue dun hackle fibers
Body . . . . Cream fox dubbing
Hackle . . . . Light blue dun

Borcher Special

Hook . . . . Mustad 94840; 10 -18
Thread . . . . Black 6/0
Wing . . . . Blue dun hen-hackle tips
Tail . . . . Mahogany ringneck pheasant tail fibers
Body . . . . Mottled turkey wing-quill fibers,
wrapped herl-style
Hackle . . . . Brown and grizzly, mixed

Ginger Fox

Hook . . . . TMC 100; 12-16
Thread . . . . Tan 6/0
Wing . . . . Mallard flank fibers
Tail . . . . Ginger hackle fibers
Underbody . . . . White poly yarn
Body . . . . Red fox dubbing
Hackle . . . . Golden ginger

Little Marryat

Hook . . . . Mustad 94840; 10-18
Thread . . . . Cream 6/0
Wing . . . . Natural gray duck quill segment
Tail . . . . Brown hackle fibers
Body . . . . Light gray rabbit dubbing
Hackle . . . . Brown

Rio Grande King

Hook . . . . TMC 100; 10-18
Thread . . . . Brown 6/0
Wing . . . . White duck quill segments
Tail . . . . Golden pheasant tippets
Body . . . . Black chenille
Hackle . . . . Brown

Adams Irresistible

Hook . . . . Mustad 94840; 8-14
Thread . . . . Black 3/0
Wing . . . . Grizzly hen-hackle tips
Tail . . . . Moose mane
Body . . . . Gray deer hair, spun and clipped
Hackle . . . . Brown and grizzly, mixed

Royal Humpy

Hook . . . . Mustad 94840; 8-14
Thread . . . . Red 6/0
Wing . . . . . . White calf body or natural deer hair
Tail . . . . Natural deer hair
Shellback . . . . Natural deer hair
Body . . . . Red floss
Hackle . . . . Brown

Coffin Fly

Hook . . . . Mustad 94840; 12-14
Thread . . . . White 6/0
Wing . . . . Teal flank
Tail . . . . Peccary or moose-mane fibers
Rib . . . . White thread
Underbody . . . . White poly yarn
Body . . . . White saddle hackle, palmered
             over white poly yarn and trimmed
Hackle . . . . Badger-colored hackle

Western Green Drake

Hook . . . . TMC 100; 10-12
Thread . . . . Olive 6/0
Wing . . . . Moose body hair
Tail . . . . Moose body hair
Rib . . . . Olive floss
Body . . . . Olive rabbit dubbing
Hackle . . . . Olive grizzly

Brown Drake

Hook . . . . Mustad 94840; 6-16
Thread . . . . Brown 6/0
Tail . . . . Brown hackle fibers
Body . . . . . Dark yellow rabbit or poly dubbing
Wing . . . . Dun turkey flats, hackle-point style
Hackle . . . . Yellow grizzly

Moose-mane Adams

Hook . . . . TMC 100; 8-16
Thread . . . . Gray 6/0
Wing . . . . Grizzly hen-hackle tips
Tail . . . . Moose mane
Body . . . . Medium gray dubbing
Hackle . . . . Brown and grizzly, mixed

White Wulff

Hook . . . . Mustad 94840; 6-16
Thread . . . . White 6/0
Wing . . . . White calf body hair
Tail . . . . White calf body hair
Body . . . . White rabbit dubbing
Hackle . . . . Cream or badger

Gray Wulff

Hook . . . . Mustad 94840; 8-14
Thread . . . . Black 6/0
Wing . . . . Natural brown bucktail
Tail . . . . Natural brown bucktail
Body . . . . Gray muskrat dubbing
Hackle . . . . Medium blue dun

Grizzly Wulff

Hook . . . . Mustad 94840; 8-14
Thread . . . . Black 6/0
Wing . . . . Natural brown bucktail
Tail . . . . Natural brown bucktail
Body . . . . Yellow floss
Hackle . . . . Brown and grizzly, mixed

Royal Wulff

Hook . . . . Mustad 94840; 8-14
Thread . . . . Black 6/0
Wing . . . . White calf tail
Tail . . . . Natural brown bucktail
Body . . . . Peacock herl with red floss band
Hackle . . . . Coachman brown

Ausable Wulff

Hook . . . . Mustad 94840; 8-14
Thread . . . . Red 6/0
Wing . . . . White calf body hair
Tail . . . . Moose body hair
Body . . . . Bleached Australian opossum
Hackle . . . . Brown and grizzly, mixed

Tent-wing Caddis

Hook. TMC 100; 12-20
Thread . . . . Tan 6/0
Body . . . . Ringneck pheasant tail fibers, wrapped herl-style
Hackle . . Dark ginger, trimmed top and bottom
Wing . . . . . Mottled turkey wing-quill segment

Hemingway Caddis

Hook . . . . Mustad 94840; 12-20
Thread . . . . Olive 6/0
Body . . . . Medium olive rabbit dubbing
Palmered hackle . . . . . Medium blue dun hackle
Underwing. . . . . Lemon wood duck flank fibers
Wing . . . . . . Gray duck quill segment, tent-style
Thorax . . . . Peacock herl
Hackle . . . . Medium blue dun, over thorax

Henryville Special

Hook. . . . . Mustad 94840; 12-20
Thread. . . . . Black 6/0
Body . . . . Olive floss
Palmered hackle . . . . Grizzly, undersized
Underwing . . . . Lemon wood duck flank fibers
Wing . . . . Two natural gray duck quill segments, tent-style
Hackle. . . . . Dark ginger

Elk-Hair Caddis

Hook. . . . . TMC 100; 10-20
Thread . . . . Tan 6/0
Body . . . . Tan rabbit dubbing
Hackle . . . . Ginger, palmered
Wing. . . . . Tan elk hair

Peacock Caddis

Hook . . . . Mustad 94840; 8-14
Thread . . . . Black 6/0
Body . . . . Peacock herl
Wing . . . . Tan elk hair
Hackle . . . . Brown and grizzly, mixed

Goddard Caddis

Hook. . . . . Mustad 94840; 10-16
Thread. . . . . Black 6/0
Body . . . . Gray deer hair, spun and clipped
Hackle. . . . . Brown
Antennae. . . . . . . Brown hackle stems, stripped and tied in at head

Deschutes Caddis

Hook. . . . . Mustad 94840; 8-12
Thread . . . . Brown 6/0
Tail . . . . Natural deer hair
Body. . . . . Yellow rabbit or poly dubbing
Wing. . . . . Light brown deer hair
Hackle . . . . Dark ginger

Delta-wing Caddis

Hook . . . . Mustad 94840; 10-22
Thread . . . . Gray 6/0
Body . . . . Gray rabbit dubbing
Wing . . . . Blue dun hen-hackle tips
Hackle . . . . Bronze dun

Small Dun Caddis

Hook. . . . . TMC 101; 16-22
Thread. . . . . Gray 6/0
Body . . . . Gray rabbit dubbing
Wing . . . . Mallard flank
Hackle. . . . . Grizzly

Slow-water Caddis

Hook . . . . TMC 100; 12-20
Thread . . . . Olive 6/0
Wing . . . . . Dun hen-hackle feathers, lacquered
Body . . . . Medium olive dubbing
Hackle . . . . Ginger
Tag . . . . Red thread

King's River

Hook . . . . Mustad 94840; 12-18
Thread . . . . Dark brown 6/0
Body . . . . Tannish brown rabbit dubbing
Wing . . . . . Mottled turkey wing-quill segment
Hackle . . . . Brown

Rio Grande Trude

Hook . . . . Mustad 94840; 10-16
Thread . . . . Black 6/0
Tail . . . . Golden pheasant tippet
Body . . . . Black rabbit dubbing
Wing . . . . White calf tail
Hackle . . . . Dark coachman brown

Little Yellow Stone

Hook . . . . Mustad 94840; 12-16
Thread . . . . Yellow 6/0
Tail . . . . Yellow deer hair
Tag . . . . Red thread
Palmered hackle . . Ginger, palmered over body
Body . . . . Yellow floss
Wing . . . . Yellow deer hair
Hackle . . . . Ginger

Black Stimulator

Hook . . . . TMC 200R; 6-8
Thread . . . . Fluorescent orange 6/0
Tail . . . . Black elk hair
Rib . . . Fine gold wire and dark blue dun hackle
Body . . . Black goat dubbing; or blend of black,
           purple, claret, rust and orange goat
Wing . . . . Black elk hair, caddis-style
Hackle . . . . Grizzly, wrapped over thorax
Thorax . . . . . Fluorescent fire-orange dubbing

Sofa Pillow

Hook . . . . Mustad 9672; 4-10
Thread . . . . Brown 6/0
Tail . . . . Red goose quill segment
Body . . . . Red floss
Wing . . . . Red fox squirrel tail fibers
Hackle . . . . Brown saddle hackle

Tan CDC/Elk Caddis

Hook . . . . TMC 100; 10-20
Thread . . . . Tan 6/0
Rib . . . . Fine gold tinsel
Body . . . . Tan rabbit dubbing
Underwing . . . . Tan CDC
Wing . . . . . Elk hair, butts trimmed to form head
Antennae . . . . Stripped ginger hackle stems

Olive CDC/Elk Caddis

Hook . . . . TMC 100; 10-20
Thread . . . . Olive 6/0
Rib . . . . Fine gold tinsel
Body . . . . Olive rabbit dubbing
Underwing . . . . Olive CDC
Wing . . . . . Elk hair, butts trimmed to form head
Antenna . . . . Stripped olive hackle stems

Gray CDC Caddis

Hook . . . . Mustad 94840; 12-20
Thread . . . . Gray 6/0
Tail . . . . Dun hackle fibers, forked
Body . . . . Gray muskrat dubbing
Wing . . Gray CDC with two grizzly hackle tips
Sides . . . . Rust CDC

Cream Midge

Hook . . . . TMC 100; 18-28
Thread . . . . White 6/0
Tail . . . . Cream hackle fibers
Body . . . . Cream rabbit dubbing
Hackle . . . . Cream

Black Midge

Hook . . . . TMC 100; 20-26
Thread . . . . Black 6/0
Tail . . . . Black hackle fibers
Body . . . . Black rabbit dubbing
Hackle . . . . Black

Griffith's Gnat

Hook . . . . Mustad 94840; 18-28
Thread . . . . Olive 6/0
Rib . . . . . . Fine gold wire, wrapped over body
and hackle
Hackle . . . . . Grizzly hackle, palmered over body
Body . . . . Peacock herl

Trico Spinner

Hook . . . . TMC 100; 20-26
Thread . . . . Black 6/0
Tail . . . . Dun hackle fibers, forked
Body . . . . Black dubbing
Wing . . . . White hen-hackle tips, spent

Rusty Spinner

Hook . . . . TMC 100; 12-24
Thread . . . . Black 6/0
Tail . . . . Medium dun hackle fibers
Body . . . . Rusty brown rabbit dubbing
Wing . . . . . . Light gray hen-hackle tips, spent

Red Quill Spinner

Hook . . . . Mustad 94833; 14-24
Thread . . . . Tan 6/0
Tail . . . . Brown hackle fibers
Body . . . . Stripped brown hackle stem
Wing . . . . Light dun hen-hackle tips, spent

Mahogany Dun Thorax

Hook . . . . Mustad 94840; 12-16
Thread . . . . Brown 6/0
Tail . . . . Brown hackle fibers
Body . . . . Mahogany rabbit dubbing
Wing . . . . Blue dun turkey flats,
upright
Hackle . . . . . . Brown hackle, clipped on bottom

Cream Thorax

Hook . . . . Mustad 94840; 12-20
Thread . . . . Cream 6/0
Tail . . . . Cream hackle fibers
Body . . . . Cream rabbit dubbing
Wing . . . . White turkey flats,
upright
Hackle . . . . . . Cream hackle, clipped on bottom

Olive Thorax

Hook . . . . Mustad 94840; 12-20
Thread . . . . Olive 6/0
Tail . . . . Blue dun hackle fibers
Body . . . . Olive rabbit dubbing
Wing . . . . Dun turkey flats,
upright
Hackle . . . . Blue dun, clipped on bottom

Brown No-hackle

Hook . . . . TMC 5230; 14-20
Thread . . . . Brown 6/0
Tail. . . . . Brown hackle fibers, forked
Body . . . . Brown rabbit dubbing
Wing . . . . Dark mallard quill segments

Olive No-hackle

Hook . . . . TMC 5230; 14-20
Thread . . . . Olive 6/0
Tail . . . . Light dun hackle fibers, forked
Body . . . . Olive dubbing
Wing . . . . Natural gray duck quill segments

Comparadun

Hook . . . . Mustad 94840; 14-20
Thread . . . . Tan 6/0
Tail . . . . Brown hackle fibers
Body . . . . Tan dubbing
Wing . . . . Elk or deer body hair

Goplin Orange Julius

Hook . . . . Mustad 94840; 12-18
Thread . . . . Cream 6/0
Tail. . . . . Light dun hackle fibers
Abdomen. . . . . Cream and yellow dubbing
Wing . . . . Cream turkey flat, folded and upright
Thorax . . . . Orange ostrich herl
Hackle . . . . Light dun

CDC Tailwater Dun

Hook . . . . Mustad 94840; 14-20
Thread . . . . Olive 6/0
Tail . . . . Dun hackle fibers
Body . . . . Olive dubbing
Wing . . . . Dun CDC
Sides . . . . Poly yarn
Thorax . . . . Olive

CDC Biot Comparadun

Hook . . . . Mustad 94840; 14-20
Thread . . . . Gray 6/0
Tail. . . . . Dun hackle fibers
Body . . . . Brown goose biot
Wing . . . . Mallard flank fibers
Thorax . . . . Gray dubbing
Hackle . . . . Dun CDC

Peacock Midge

Hook . . . . Mustad 94840; 14-18
Thread . . . . Black 6/0
Tail. . . . . Grizzly or red hackle fibers
Body . . . . Peacock herl
Hackle . . . . Grizzly

Trico Parachute

Hook . . . . TMC 101; 20-24
Thread . . . . White 6/0
Tail . . . . Grizzly hackle fibers
Body . . . . White floss or thread
Wing . . . White hen-hackle tips, parachute-style
Thorax . . . . Black rabbit dubbing
Hackle . . . . Grizzly dun, parachute-style

Morris May Dark

Hook . . . . Mustad 94840; 8-20
Thread . . . . Dark brown 6/0
Tail . . . . Ginger hackle fibers
Abdomen. . . . . Brown poly yarn
Wing . . . . Gray poly yarn
Thorax . . . . Brown poly dubbing
Hackle . . . . Brown, wrapped over thorax

Wet Flies

A fly angler who took up the sport twenty years ago may never have fished a traditional wet-fly pattern. The fancy patterns of the late 1800s and early 1900s have all but disappeared from most fly shops and catalogs. Yet wet flies were the most popular patterns in America until the 1950s.

Traditional wet flies had colorful names like "Queen of the Waters" and "Wickham's Fancy" and were meant to be fished below the surface to suggest a variety of drowned mayflies. Most were attractor patterns with plenty of flash and color.

Wet flies went out of fashion as more realistic patterns, such as nymphs and dry flies, gained popularity. But wets didn't disappear entirely, and for good reason: they still catch fish.

Today, wet flies are making a comeback. Traditional wet flies like the Parmachene Belle and Wooly Worm (left) remain popular with flytiers and anglers, and the soft-hackle fly, a wet-fly/nymph hybrid developed in England, has found wide acceptance in America.

Though closely related, traditional wet flies and soft-hackle flies differ somewhat in the way they are tied. Wet flies often resemble dry-fly patterns with hackle and wings sloping back over a dubbed body.

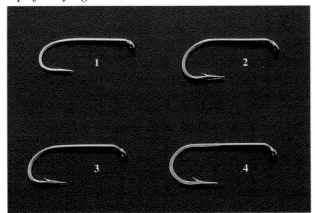

POPULAR HOOKS include: (1) TMC 3761; (2) Mustad 3366, (3) 3906 and (4) 7957.

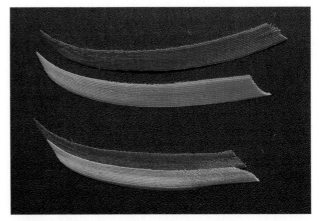

MARRY quill segments of different feathers by stroking edges to interlock barbules, making a multicolor wing.

QUILL-SEGMENT wings for wet flies can be tied in with tips curving up or down to create a different look.

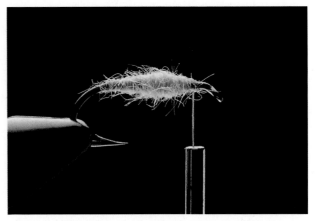

DUB wet-fly bodies to cigar shape. This way, tapered front end allows wings and hackle to slope back.

Soft-hackle flies seldom have wings and are more sparsely tied. They have a tightly dubbed body, and hackle made of partridge, hen or other soft-fibered feathers.

Wet and soft-hackle flies are most effective when fished unweighted on a dead-drift, or as a dropper fly rigged several inches below a dry.

Another type of wet fly is the salmon fly. These complex and beautiful fly patterns are related to both wet flies and streamers, but make up a distinct fly category.

Some salmon flies have elaborate and colorful feather wings. Called *fully dressed*, these patterns rarely see water. They are usually tied for the purpose of display and feature married wings (above). Often made of exotic and hard-to-find materials, fully dressed flies are considered the pinnacle of the flytier's art.

One of the most popular of the traditional wet-fly patterns is the Light Cahill (right, and following pages). It imitates a number of major midseason mayfly species on rivers from Maine to Minnesota.

Created in the 1880s by Dan Cahill, in upstate New York, this fly has a light coloration, making it an ideal pattern for mornings, evenings or any low-light situations. It is also tied in a dry-fly version (p. 96).

The Light Cahill

How to Tie a Wet Fly:
The Light Cahill

How to Tie a Wet Fly: The Light Cahill

Recipe	
Hook	TMC 3761; 10-16
Thread	Cream 6/0
Tail . . .	Lemon wood duck flank fibers
Body	Cream rabbit dubbing
Hackle	Cream hen or rooster saddle
Wing	Lemon wood duck flank fibers

How to Tie the Light Cahill

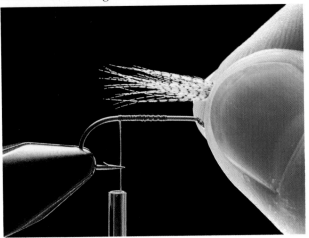

1 Start thread at midpoint of shank and wind back to bend. Strip a small bunch of wood duck flank fibers, or substitute, for tail. Stack fibers so tips are aligned. Length of tail should equal length of hook shank.

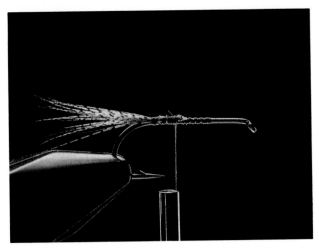

2 Tie in tail at hook bend with several soft loops. Trim off excess butt ends.

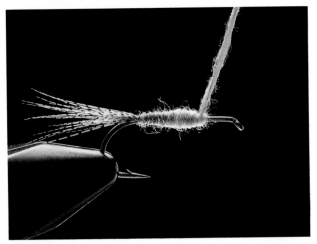

3 Apply a small amount of dubbing to thread and wrap dubbed thread forward to about one-third shank length behind eye.

4 Select a dark cream rooster saddle hackle. Fold hackle by stroking hackle fibers between fingers.

106

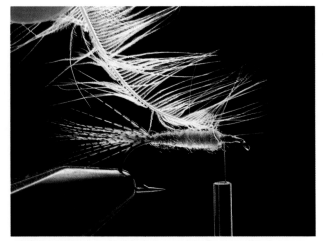

5 Tie in tip of folded saddle hackle with fibers facing back. Secure with several turns of thread, and trim off excess tip.

6 Begin winding hackle around shank. Stroke fibers back with fingers after first wrap.

7 Make two more wraps, and secure hackle stem with several turns of thread. Trim off hackle fibers that lie over top of body so wing will lie flat.

8 Gather tips of folded wood duck flank feather to make wing. Finished wing should be $1\frac{1}{2}$ times hook-shank length.

9 Tie in wing on top of hook with several soft loops, and make a few more wraps to secure.

10 Trim butt end of flank feather. Wrap thread forward and form head. Whip-finish, and apply head cement.

Catalog of Wet Flies

Alder
Hook . . . . TMC 3761; 10-14
Thread . . . . Black 6/0
Tag . . . . Fine flat gold tinsel
Body . . . . Peacock herl
Hackle . . . . Black hen
Wing . . . . Mottled turkey quill segments

Blue Dun
Hook . . . . TMC 3761; 10-16
Thread . . . . Gray 6/0
Tail . . . . Medium blue dun hackle fibers
Body . . . . Muskrat dubbing
Hackle . . . . Medium blue dun hen
Wing . . . . Natural gray duck quill segments

Cow Dung
Hook . . . . TMC 3761; 10-16
Thread . . . . Black 6/0
Tag . . . . Fine flat gold tinsel
Body . . . . Dark olive floss
Hackle . . . . Brown hen
Wing . . . . Cinnamon turkey quill segment

Orvis Light Cahill
Hook . . . . TMC 3761; 10-16
Thread . . . . Cream 6/0
Tail . . . . Cream hackle fibers
Body . . . . Cream rabbit dubbing
Hackle . . . . Cream hen
Wing . . . . Lemon wood duck flank fibers

Dark Cahill
Hook . . . . TMC 3761; 10-16
Thread . . . . Black 6/0
Tail . . . . Lemon wood duck flank fibers
Body . . . . Muskrat dubbing
Hackle . . . . Dark ginger hen
Wing . . . . Lemon wood duck flank fibers

Dark Hendrickson
Hook . . . . TMC 3761; 10-16
Thread . . . . Black 6/0
Tail . . . . Medium blue dun
Body . . . . Muskrat dubbing
Hackle . . . . Medium blue dun hen
Wing . . . . Lemon wood duck flank fibers

Quill Gordon
Hook . . . . TMC 3761; 10-16
Thread . . . . Black 6/0
Tail . . . . Medium blue dun hackle fibers
Body . . . . . . Stripped peacock stem, quill-style
Hackle . . . . Medium blue dun hen
Wing . . . . Lemon wood duck flank fibers

American March Brown
Hook . . . . TMC 3761; 10-14
Thread . . . . Black 6/0
Tail . . . . Mottled grouse hackle fibers
Rib . . . . Yellow thread or oval gold tinsel
Body . . . . Grayish tan rabbit dubbing
Hackle . . . . Mottled grouse
Wing . . . . Mottled turkey quill segments

Hornberg
Hook . . . . Mustad 9672; 6-10
Thread . . . . Black 6/0
Body . . . . Flat silver tinsel
Underwing . . . . Yellow calf tail
Wing . . . . Mallard flank feathers,
one on each side
Cheeks . . . . Jungle cock
Hackle . . . . Grizzly

Professor

Hook	TMC 3761; 10-16
Thread	Black 6/0
Tail	Red hackle fibers
Rib	Fine gold flat tinsel
Body	Yellow dubbing or floss
Hackle	Brown hen
Wing	Mallard flank fibers

Parmachene Belle

Hook	TMC 3761; 10-16
Thread	Black 6/0
Tail	Red and white hackle fibers, mixed
Rib	Fine gold flat tinsel
Body	Yellow floss
Hackle	Red hen and white hen, mixed
Wing	Married sections of red and white duck quill segments

Royal Coachman

Hook	TMC 3761; 10-16
Thread	Black 6/0
Tail	Golden pheasant tippet fibers
Rib	Fine gold wire
Body	Peacock herl with red floss band
Hackle	Dark brown hen
Wing	White duck quill segments

Leadwing Coachman

Hook	TMC 3761; 6-16
Thread	Black 6/0
Tip	Fine gold flat tinsel
Body	Peacock herl
Hackle	Brown hen
Wing	Natural gray duck quill segments

Black Gnat

Hook	TMC 3761; 10-14
Thread	Black 6/0
Tail	Black hackle fibers
Body	Black rabbit dubbing
Hackle	Black hen
Wing	Natural gray duck quill segment

Pheasant Tail

Hook	TMC 3761; 10-16
Thread	Olive 6/0
Rib	Fine copper wire
Body	Pheasant tail fibers, wrapped herl-style
Hackle	Brown partridge

Partridge and Yellow

Hook	TMC 3761; 10-16
Thread	Yellow 6/0
Abdomen	Yellow floss
Thorax	Natural rabbit dubbing
Hackle	Brown partridge or mallard flank

Tup's Indispensable

Hook	TMC 3761; 10-16
Thread	Yellow 6/0
Tail	Blue dun hen-hackle fibers
Body	Yellow floss
Thorax	Light pink rabbit dubbing
Hackle	Blue dun hen

Yellow Wooly Worm

Hook	TMC 3761; 2-12
Thread	Black 6/0
Tail	Red hackle fibers
Rib	Fine silver wire
Body	Yellow chenille
Hackle	Grizzly, palmered

Rusty Rat

Hook	TMC 7999; 2-10
Thread	Red 6/0
Tag	Fine gold oval tinsel
Tail	Peacock sword fibers
Rib	Gold oval tinsel
Body	Rear half, yellow floss; front half, peacock herl
Wing	Gray fox guard hair
Cheeks	Jungle cock (optional)
Hackle	Grizzly

Cosseboom

Hook	TMC 7999; 2-10
Thread	Red 6/0
Tag	Silver flat tinsel
Tail	Medium olive floss
Rib	Silver flat tinsel
Body	Medium olive floss
Wing	Gray squirrel tail
Hackle	Lemon yellow

Hairy Mary

Hook	Mustad 36890; 4-10
Thread	Black 6/0
Tag	Gold oval tinsel
Tail	Golden pheasant crest
Rib	Gold oval tinsel
Body	Black floss
Beard	Bright blue hackle fibers
Wing	Brown fitch (fur) tail fibers

Red Abbey

Hook	Mustad 36890; 4-10
Thread	Black 6/0
Head	Black or Red
Tag	Silver oval tinsel
Tail	Red goose quill segment or bucktail
Rib	Silver flat or oval tinsel
Body	Red floss or wool yarn
Beard	Brown hackle, pulled down
Wing	Light brown squirrel tail hair, or brown bucktail
Cheeks	Jungle cock (optional)

Black Dose

Hook	Mustad 36890; 4-10
Thread	Black 6/0
Tag	Silver oval tinsel
Butt	Pale yellow floss
Tail	Golden pheasant crest, covered half its length by red hackle fibers
Rib	Silver oval tinsel
Body	Black floss
Wing	Four peacock sword fibers, and bundle of black bear fibers
Beard	Black hen hackle
Cheeks	Jungle cock (optional)

Undertaker

Hook	TMC 7999; 2-10
Thread	Black 6/0
Tag	Fine gold flat tinsel
Butt	Rear half, fluorescent green floss; front half, fluorescent orange floss
Rib	Gold oval tinsel
Body	Peacock herl
Beard	Black hackle
Wing	Black bear hair

Jock Scott

Hook . . . . TMC 36890; 5/0-6
Thread . . . . Black 6/0
Tag. . . . . Flat silver tinsel and yellow floss
Tail. . . Golden pheasant crest, covered half its length with orange hackle
Butt . . . . Black ostrich herl
Body . . . . Rear half, yellow silk floss ribbed with small silver tinsel;
front half, black silk floss ribbed with medium silver tinsel;
toucan, tied in above and below hook at midpoint of shank
Hackle . . . . Black hackle over black floss section of body
Beard . . . . Gallina or black hen hackle
Wing . . . . Two strips of black turkey with white tips, golden pheasant tail,
bustard, gray mallard, peacock sword fibers, blue swan,
yellow and red macaw, bronze mallard
Topping . . . . Golden pheasant crest
Sides . . . . Jungle cock
Cheeks . . . . Blue chatterer and blue macaw

Black Doctor

Hook . . . . TMC 36890; 5/0-6
Thread . . . . Black 6/0
Tag. . . . . Silver thread, yellow floss
Tail. . . . . Golden pheasant crest and Indian crow
Butt . . . . Scarlet wool
Body . . . . Black floss
Rib . . . . Silver oval tinsel
Hackle . . . . Dark claret
Beard . . . . Speckled gallina or hen
Wing . . . . Golden pheasant tippet and crest strands; peacock wing;
married strands of scarlet, blue and yellow swan, florican, bustard;
light mottled turkey tail; married strips of teal and
narrow strips of brown mallard
Topping . . . . Golden pheasant crest
Head . . . . Scarlet wool

Gordon

Hook . . . . TMC 36890; 5/0-6
Thread . . . . Black 6/0
Tag. . . . . Flat silver tinsel and yellow floss
Tail. . . . . Golden pheasant crest and tippet
Butt . . . . Black ostrich herl
Body . . . . Rear one-third, yellow floss; front two-thirds, claret floss
Rib . . . . Silver oval tinsel and silver flat tinsel
Hackle . . . . Claret hackle, palmered over claret floss
Beard . . . . Blue hackle
Wing . . . . . Pair of golden pheasant sword feathers; yellow, blue and red
swan; bustard; Lady Amherst pheasant tail
Topping . . . . Golden pheasant crest
Cheeks . . . . Jungle cock

Terrestrials

But don't be afraid to try a terrestrial pattern in early and late season as well. Terrestrials such as ants and beetles are a staple in a trout's diet throughout the season, and their imitations can be used as searching patterns when no insects are emerging.

Even during a heavy mayfly hatch, some trout will rise to terrestrials that drift into their feeding window.

Cast a terrestrial along the bank or shoreline. Twitch it occasionally to make it look like a struggling insect. This will draw fish from farther away than will a fly drifting motionless.

When the hot summer winds blow across the water, trout feed heavily on the increasing numbers of land insects, or *terrestrials*, that accidently fall, or are blown into, lakes and streams. Then, a well-tied terrestrial imitation can be extremely productive.

Success with terrestrial imitations isn't limited to trout fishing. Panfish and bass will readily take a hopper or cricket pattern twitched on the surface of a lake or farm pond.

How to Make Legs for Hoppers and Crickets

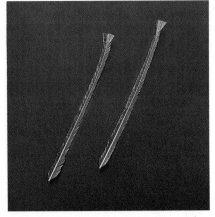

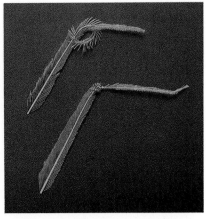

1 Select two large hackle feathers.

2 Trim off ends of fibers, leaving ⅛-inch stubs along stem.

3 Tie an overhand knot in middle of stem to form leg joint. Crimp stem ⅛ inch from end to form foot.

Tips for Tying Terrestrials

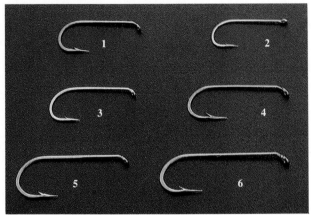

POPULAR HOOKS include: (1) Mustad 94840; (2) TMC 101; (3) Mustad 94833, and (4) 9671; (5) TMC 100 and (6) Mustad 9672.

ADD a small piece of fluorescent yarn, or *indicator,* to the top of a terrestrial pattern so you can see it more easily.

Terrestrial types include:

Ants. These small insects make up a large percentage of the natural terrestrials that find their way into the water. Trout feed on ants whenever they are available, making imitations effective from early spring through late fall.

Hoppers and Crickets. Although they represent only a small percentage of a fish's diet, hoppers and crickets are commonly taken by trout, panfish and bass, especially in late summer. Many terrestrial patterns are tied complete with legs (above).

Beetles. The opportunistic trout will rise to a beetle even in winter, making beetle imitations year-round producers. Imitations are tied using deer hair or foam bodies, often with a small piece of fluorescent yarn (above).

One of the most effective terrestrial patterns is the Deer-hair Beetle (below, and following pages). Tied with dyed deer hair over a body of peacock herl, this pattern is easy to tie, floats well and consistently catches fish all season long.

The Deer-hair Beetle

Recipe	
Hook	Mustad 94840; 10 - 16
Thread	Black 3/0
Shellback	Black deer hair
Body	Peacock herl

How to Tie the Deer-hair Beetle

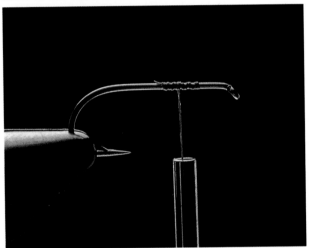

1 Start thread at middle of hook shank.

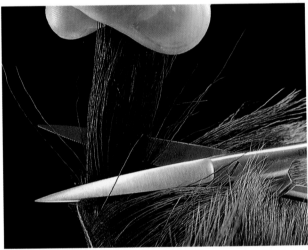

2 Snip a small bundle of deer hair, about the diameter of a pencil.

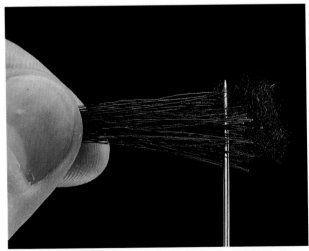

3 Hold deer hair by tips, and comb out short underfur with dubbing needle.

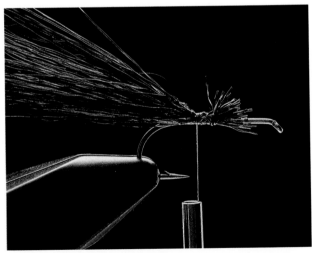

4 Tie in butt ends of deer hair at middle of hook shank, with tips facing back. Don't be concerned if butts flare slightly; wind thread over them to secure.

5 Trim any excess butts, then wind thread back to hook bend.

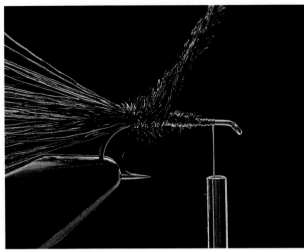

6 Tie in two or three strands of herl and trim butt ends. Wind thread forward to ⅛ inch behind eye.

7 Wrap herl forward around shank and secure with several turns of thread. Trim excess herl.

8 Bring tips of deer hair forward over herl and tie in just behind eye to form *shellback*. Make several firm wraps with thread, and whip-finish.

9 Trim off excess tips to form head of beetle.

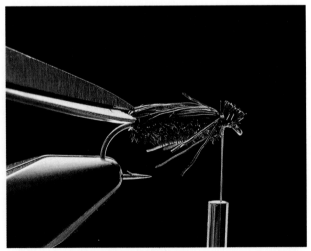

10 Snip one or two strands from each side of rear of body to form legs. Apply head cement.

Catalog of Terrestrials

Black Fur Ant

Hook . . . . TMC 100; 14-20
Thread . . . . Black 6/0
Abdomen . . . . Black rabbit dubbing
Hackle . . . . Black
Thorax . . . . Black rabbit dubbing

Foam Ant

Hook . . . . TMC 100; 14-20
Thread . . . . Black 6/0
Abdomen . . . . Black foam
Hackle . . . . CDC feathers
Indicator . . . . Yellow foam
Legs . . . . Black Krystal Flash
Thorax . . . . Black foam
Antennae . . . . Black Krystal Flash

Flying Ant

Hook . . . . TMC 100; 14-18
Thread . . . . Black 6/0
Abdomen . . . . Black rabbit dubbing
Wing . . . . Mallard quill segment, tent-style
Legs . . . . Moose-mane fibers
Hackle . . . . Black hackle
Thorax . . . . Black rabbit dubbing

Black Beetle

Hook . . . . TMC 100; 14-20
Thread . . . . Black 6/0
Shellback . . . . Black deer hair, pulled over
body and clipped to form legs and head
Body . . . . Black wool yarn or peacock herl

Foam Cricket

Hook . . . . , ... TMC 100; 8-14
Thread . . . . Black 6/0
Abdomen . . . . Black foam
Thorax . . . . Foam tied at eye
Legs . . . . Black goose biots and black Krystal Flash
Antennae . . . . Black Krystal Flash

CDC Peacock Beetle

Hook . . . . TMC 100; 14-16
Thread . . . . Black 6/0
Shellback . . . . Black CDC feathers
Body . . . . Peacock herl
Legs . . . . Black CDC feathers
Head . . . . Butts from shellback, trimmed

Dave's Cricket

Hook . . . . Mustad 94833; 6-12
Thread . . . . Black 6/0
Tail . . . . Black deer hair and brown yarn
Body . . . . Brown yarn
Hackle . . . . Black hackle, palmered and clipped
Wing . . . . . Black goose quill segment, tent-style
Legs . . . . Black hackle stems, trimmed
and knotted
Collar . . . . Black deer hair
Head . . . . Black deer hair, spun and clipped

Henry's Fork Cricket

Hook . . . . Mustad 94833; 6-16
Thread . . . . Brown 6/0
Body . . . . Brown deer hair
Wing . . . . Black hen saddle, lacquered
Head . . . . . . Black elk hair, tied with tips facing
forward, then pulled back
Legs . . . . Black rubber, knotted

Green Leaf Hopper

Hook . . . . TMC 100; 16-22
Thread . . . . White 6/0
Body . . . . White thread
Hackle . . . . . Insect green hackle, palmered over
body, clipped top and bottom
Wing . . . . Insect green mallard flank, lacquered

Letort Hopper

Hook . . . . Mustad 94833; 8-16
Thread . . . . Gray 6/0
Body . . . . Yellow rabbit dubbing
Wing . . . . Mottled turkey quill segment
Overwing. . . . . Natural deer hair
Head . . . . . Natural deer hair, spun and clipped

Rubber Legs Henry's Fork Hopper

Hook. . . . . Mustad 94833; 8-12
Thread . . . . Yellow 6/0
Body . . . . White deer hair
Rib . . . . Yellow thread
Underwing . . . . Yellow elk hair
Wing . . . . Speckled hen saddle, lacquered
Head . . . Elk hair, tied in with tips facing forward,
              then pulled back to form head and collar
Legs . . . . Rubber leg material, knotted

Joe's Hopper

Hook . . . . Mustad 94833; 6-14
Thread . . . . Black 6/0
Tail. . . . . Red hackle fibers
Butt and body . . . . Yellow poly foam
Palmered hackle . . . . . . Brown hackle, clipped
Wings. . . . . Mottled turkey quill segment
Hackle . . . . Brown and grizzly, mixed

Dave's Hopper

Hook . . . . Mustad 94833; 4-12
Thread . . . . Gray 6/0
Tail. . . . . Red deer hair and yellow yarn
Body . . . . Yellow yarn
Hackle . . . . Brown, palmered and clipped
Underwing. . . . . Yellow calf tail
Wing . . . Turkey wing-quill segment, lacquered
Legs. . . . . Yellow grizzly hackle stems,
                                    clipped and knotted
Collar. . . . . Natural deer hair, spun
Head . . . . . . Natural deer hair, spun and clipped

Jan's Hopper

Hook. . . . . Mustad 94833; 6-16
Thread . . . . Black 6/0
Tail . . . . Red hackle fibers, with a loop of
                                    yellow wool yarn
Body . . . . Yellow wool yarn
Rib . . . . Brown hackle, trimmed short
Wing . . . . Tan elk hair
Hackle . . . . Brown and grizzly, mixed

Parachute Hopper

Hook . . . . Mustad 94833; 8-14
Thread . . . . Tan 6/0
Wing post. . . . . White calf body, parachute-style
Body . . . . Tan rabbit dubbing
Tent wing. . . . . . . Mottled turkey quill segment
Legs. . . . Ringneck pheasant tail fibers, knotted
Hackle . . . . Grizzly, parachute-style

Jassid

Hook . . . . TMC 101; 16-24
Thread. . . . . Black 6/0
Body . . . . Black thread
Hackle . . . . Ginger, palmered over body,
                                    trimmed on bottom
Wing . . . . Single jungle cock feather

Inchworm

Hook. . . . . Mustad 94840; 10-14
Thread . . . . Green 3/0
Body . . Green bucktail, tied in at eye, extending
            back over bend, with thread wrapped
            open spiral over entire length
Indicator . . . . Fire orange yarn

Caterpillar

Hook . . . . Mustad 9672; 6-8
Thread . . . . Black 3/0
Rear hackle . . . . Grizzly
Rib. . . . . Silver wire
Overbody. . . . . . Peacock herl, tied in over back
Body . . . . Yellow floss
Front hackle. Grizzly

Bass & Pike Flies

Anglers across the country are discovering the thrill of catching bass, pike and even muskie on big artificial flies.

Most bass and pike flies imitate some kind of aquatic foods, such as minnows, frogs, crayfish, mice, leeches, worms and, occasionally, large insects. Other patterns rely on flash, color and noise to provoke an aggressive response.

The keys to tying effective bass and pike patterns are size, color and action.

SIZE. Select a fly suitable for the size fish you are after. Smallmouth bass generally prefer 2- to 3-inch flies; largemouth, 3- to 5- inch. Pike and muskie, which often pursue baitfish one-fourth their own length, will often take a fly up to ten inches.

COLOR. In general, flies for clear water should be more subdued than those for murky water. But many fly fishermen prefer white or yellow for surface flies; blues and violets for subsurface. Don't be afraid to experiment with a variety of color combiations to find one that works best for you.

ACTION. Spun deer hair can be trimmed to produce a popping or gurgling sound when retrieved with a quick, short, stripping action. Surface patterns are often tied with lifelike legs and tails to imitate mice, frogs or other aquatic foods.

Other patterns are designed to dive below the surface when retrieved, mimicking a struggling or injured

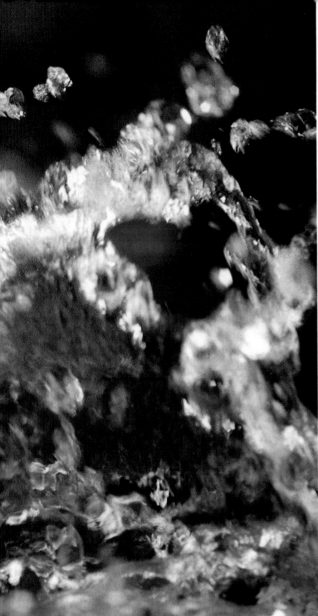

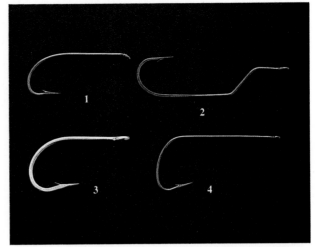

POPULAR HOOKS include: (1) Mustad 3399; (2) 79666, a weedless keel hook; (3) TMC 800S, and (4) mustad 37187.

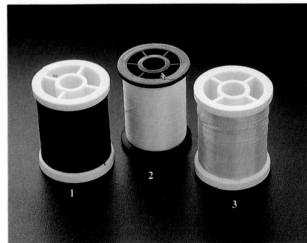

POPULAR THREADS include: (1) 2/0 Danville Plus, (2) 3/0 Monocord and (3) superstrong 1/0 Kevlar.

minnow. Subsurface patterns are often tied with long tails made of marabou, rabbit strips, hackle feathers or synthetic hair that pulses like fins or gills under water.

Some patterns, such as the Dahlberg Diver (below, and following pages), are designed to do both.

The Dahlberg Diver

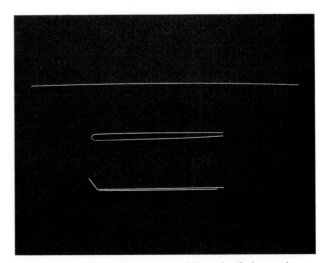

MAKE a weedguard from a 4-inch length of piano wire. Bend and crimp wire as shown, and tie in at eye after wrapping body materials so crimp covers point.

How to Tie a Bass Fly: The Dahlberg Diver

Recipe	
Hook	TMC 800S; 2-10
Thread	White 3/0
Weedguard	Heavy clear mono
Wings	Red saddle-hackle feathers
Tail	Red deer hair
Collar	Red deer hair
Head	Red deer hair, spun and clipped

How to Tie the Dahlberg Diver

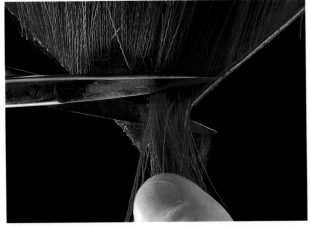

1 Start thread at hook bend and wrap down to middle of bend. Cut a 5-inch length of heavy clear monofilament for weedguard. Tie in one end of monofilament.

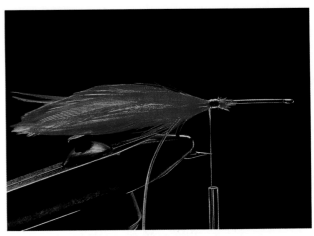

2 Select, size and prepare six saddle hackles for wings. Tie in three on each side of shank at hook bend. Hackle feathers should flare outward.

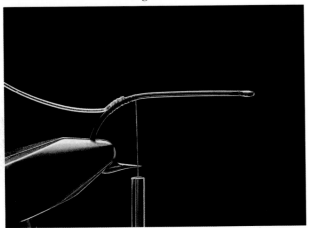

3 Snip and prepare a clump of deer body hair. Align tips in stacker.

4 Position clump of deer hair over shank directly in front of wings with tips facing back.

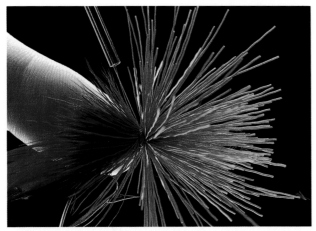

5 Make several soft loops to secure. Do not allow tips of deer hair to flare. Place finger against back side of hair while cinching to prevent it from spinning. Tips will form tail.

6 Tie in and spin second clump of hair directly in front of first. Continue adding, spinning and packing hair until shank is covered. Leave about 1/8-inch gap behind eye. Whip-finish, and trim off excess thread.

7 Turn the hook upside down in vise. Trim bottom of fly with scissors or razor blade so it is flat and level. Cut as close as possible to shank, taking care not to cut thread wraps.

8 Turn the hook right side up. Trim front half of deer hair body to bullet shape, as shown, with tips of scissors. Leave a collar of flared deer hair behind tapered head.

9 Trim ends of collar to approximately twice the radius of the body.

10 Reattach thread at hook eye. Push monofilament up through eye and fold back over head of fly. Secure with several turns of thread. Trim off butt end of mono, and whip-finish.

Catalog of Bass & Pike Flies

Deer-hair Bug

Hook. . . . . TMC 800S; 4-10
Thread . . . . Olive 3/0
Weedguard . . . . Heavy clear monofilament (optional)
Tail . . . . Yellow marabou, red and pearl Krystal Flash and two
orange grizzly saddles, each side
Sides . . . . Orange hackle, red Krystal Flash, each side
Legs . . . . Orange rubber, pearl and red Krystal Flash
Head . . . . Various colors of deer hair, spun and clipped
Eyes . . . . Plastic doll eyes, glued to head

Krazy Kicker Frog

Hook . . . . Mustad 3366; 2-10
Thread . . . . Olive 3/0
Legs . . . . . Light green bucktail, tied one-fourth shank length from bend,
bucktail wrapped with thread to form joint
Body. . . . . Light green and dark green deer hair, spun and clipped
Weedguard . . . . Heavy clear monofilament

Clauser Minnow

Hook. . . . . TMC 800S; 1/0-6
Thread . . . . Brown 3/0
Eyes . . . . Hourglass eyes, painted red with black pupils
Beard . . . . Orange bucktail
Wing . . . . Red bucktail, with copper Krystal Flash

Dave's Crayfish

Hook (upside down) . . . . TMC 300; 1/0-8
Thread . . . . Orange 3/0
Eyes . . . . Monofilament
Antennae . . . . Two dark moose body fibers
Pincers . . . . Orange speckled hen
Rib . . . . Copper wire
Hackle . . . . Orange grizzly hackle
Body. . . . . . . Burnt orange Antron yarn, picked out with dubbing needle
Shellback . . . . Orange Swiss Straw, with black waterproof markings

Rabbit Clauser

Hook. . . . . TMC 800S; 1/0-6
Thread . . . . Yellow 3/0
Body. . . . . . Red and yellow rabbit strips, glued to shank top and bottom
Legs . . . . Yellow rubber legs, pearl and red Krystal Flash
Eyes . . . . Nickel hourglass eyes
Weedguard . . . . Heavy clear monofilament (optional)

Nix's Sunfish

Hook . . . . TMC 8089; 1/0-6
Thread . . . . White 3/0
Weedguard . . . . Heavy clear monofilament (optional)
Rib . . . . Copper wire
Body. . . . . Green rabbit or Antron dubbing
Tail and Fins. . . . . Green grizzly hen saddle, tied down with ribbing
Sides . . . . Red hen-hackle tips
Head . . . . Green wool dubbing, with orange wool on underside,
trimmed to shape
Eyes . . . . Plastic doll eyes, glued to head

Dahlberg's Mega Diver

Hook	TMC 800S; 2/0-4		Collar and head	Chartreuse deer hair, spun and clipped
Thread	Chartreuse 3/0		Weedguard	Piano wire, bent to shape
Wing	Chartreuse synthetic hair with strands of gold Flashabou		Eyes	Plastic doll eyes, glued to head

Whitlock's Hairwater Pup

Hook	Mustad 36890; 2-10		Body	Purple rabbit dubbing
Thread	Purple 3/0		Beard	Purple Flashabou
Weedguard	Heavy clear monofilament		Collar	Purple deer hair
Tail	Purple rabbit fur strip		Head	Purple deer hair, spun and clipped
Rib	Fine silver wire		Eyes	Purple doll eyes

Mouserat

Hook	Mustad 37187; 2-10
Thread	Black 3/0
Weedguard	Heavy clear monofilament
Tail	Dark brown suede strip
Body	Dark deer hair, spun
Ears	Dark brown suede, cut to shape
Collar	Dark deer hair, spun
Head	Dark deer hair, spun and clipped
Whiskers	Dark moose body hair
Eyes	Black waterproof marker

Chamois Leech

Hook	TMC 7999; 1/0-6
Thread	Green 6/0
Weedguard	Heavy clear monofilament
Butt	Fluorescent orange yarn
Rib	Fine copper wire
Underbody	Brown Antron dubbing, picked out with dubbing needle
Body	Olive chamois strip over back of entire fly, left long to form tail and colored with green and black marker
Hackle	Brown speckled hen saddle
Eyes	Silver bead-chain

Dahlberg Rabbit Strip Diver

Hook	Mustad 37187; 2-10
Thread	White 3/0
Weedguard	Heavy clear monofilament
Tail	Yellow rabbit fur strip

Topping	Gold Flashabou
Collar	Yellow deer hair, spun and clipped to shape
Head	Yellow deer hair, spun and clipped

Dahlberg Skipper

Hook	TMC 800S; 2-6
Thread	White 3/0
Tail	White synthetic hair, with pearl Mylar
Sides	Red marabou
Collar and Head	White deer hair, spun and clipped
Weedguard	Piano wire, bent to shape
Eyes	Yellow doll eyes

Dahlberg Diving Bug

Hook	TMC 800S; 2-10
Thread	White 3/0
Weedguard	Heavy clear monofilament
Wing	Black marabou
Sides	Two grizzly hackles, with pearl Mylar and peacock herl
Collar	Black deer hair
Head	Black deer hair, spun and clipped

Murray's Strymph

Hook	TMC 5263; 2-10
Thread	Black 3/0
Tail	Black ostrich herl
Body	Black rabbit, thickly dubbed
Hackle	Brown hen saddle

Green Bomber

Hook	TMC 7999; 2-8
Thread	Black 3/0
Tail	White calf tail
Palmered hackle	Brown hackle, palmered through body
Body	Green deer hair, spun and clipped
Wing	White calf tail, upright-and-divided
Hackle	Brown, dry-fly style

Barr's Bouface

Hook . . . . TMC 800S; 1/0-4
Thread . . . . Black 3/0

Tail . . . . Black rabbit strip, with Mylar and Krystal Flash
Body . . . . Black marabou on top, with yellow below

Eelworm

Hook . . . . TMC 7999; 1/0-6
Thread . . . . Red 3/0
Weedguard . . . . Heavy clear monofilament
Tail. . . . . Four black saddle-hackle feathers

Body . . . . Black wool yarn
Hackle. . . . . Black, palmered over body
Eyes. . . . . Large silver bead-chain

Whitlock's Hair Worm

Hook . . . . TMC 8089; 2-10
Thread . . . . White 3/0
Weedguard . . . . Heavy clear monofilament

Tail . . . . Six-inch blue rabbit strip, tied in at eye
Body . . . . Blue rabbit strip, glued to shank and tail strip
Eyes. . . . . White doll eyes

Index

Cy DeCosse Incorporated offers
a variety of how-to books.
For information write:

Cy DeCosse Subscriber Books
5900 Green Oak Drive
Minnetonka, MN 55343